I0406880

NESARA II

National Economic Security
and Reformation Act

Maine-Patriot.com
3 Linnell Circle
Brunswick, Maine 04011

maine-patriot.com

NESARA II

NESARA II

National Economic Security and Reformation Act

Contents

Background

About NESARA -- 7
Prosperity Programs & NESARA ------------------- 39

1. Confirmation --- 43
2. The Monaco Colloquium ------------------------- 51
3. The Meeting of 57 ---------------------------------- 59
4. The White Dragon Society ----------------------- 65
5. Global Debt Forgiveness ------------------------- 67
6. 57-Nation Alliance Issues Warning -------------- 77
7. The Biggest Event! - *In 2000 Years* ------------- 81
8. Address Never Given ----------------------------139
9. Meetings With Extraterrestrials ------------------141
10. A Suggested Response -------------------------147
11. The World After NESARA ----------------------149
12. Geophysics Of The Paradigm Shift -----------153
13. Summation ---------------------------------------163

"SIC FULGET IN UMBRAS"
"TRUTH IS ENVELOPED IN OBSCURITY"

NESARA II

Background
About NESARA

Throughout history many prophets have come forth... but change is on the horizon. The power grab of the elite is coming to an end.

With all their power and money, the bankers thought themselves to be above the law. But cracks were now appearing in their foundations. Angry Americans were beginning to fight back.

A Class Action Lawsuit was brewing, which would thereafter change the balance of power. This change began in the mid 1970's when the Federal Land Bank illegally foreclosed on farmers' mortgages all throughout the Midwest. In each of these cases, the farmers were defrauded by the banks, with the approval of the Federal Reserve System. These court cases would become known as the Farmer Claims Program.

In 1978 an elderly ranch farmer in Colorado purchase a farm with a loan from the Federal Land Bank. After he died, the property was passed on to his son, Roy Schwasinger, Jr. who was a retired military General. Soon after a Federal Land Bank officer and a federal Marshal appeared on his property and informed him that the bank was foreclosing on his farm, and to vacate it within 30 days.

Without his knowledge his deceased father had signed a stipulation which reverted the property back to the Federal Land Bank in the event of the borrower's death.

Outraged, Roy Schwasinger filed a class-action lawsuit in the Denver Federal Court system. But the case didn't go very far, and the suit was dismissed for filing incorrectly. This began Roy Schwasinger's investigation into the inner workings of the banking system.

In 1982, he was given a contract by the US Senate and later the Supreme Court, to investigate banking fraud. But because he was under a strict non-disclosure order, he was not allowed to tell anyone what he had discovered.

In the late 80's he began sharing his knowledge with others, including high-ranking military personnel, who helped bring about a class-action lawsuit against the Federal Government. (CV920C-1781 93Jun.2)

The 1st series of those loses began in the 1980's when William and Shirley Baskerville, of Fort Collins, Colorado were involved in a bankruptcy case with First Interstate Bank of Fort Collins, that was trying to foreclose on their farm.

At a restaurant, their lawyer informed them that he would no longer be able to help them, and walked off. Overhearing the conversation, Roy Schwasinger offered his advice on how to appeal the case in Bankruptcy Court.

So in 1987, they filed an appeal with the United States District Court in Colorado.

On December 3rd, 1988, the Denver Federal Court System ruled that, indeed, the banks had defrauded the Baskervilles and proceeded to reverse its bankruptcy decision, but when the foreclosed property was not returned, they filed a new lawsuit. Eventually 23 other Farmers, Ranches, and Indians, swindled by the bank, in the same manner, would join in the case.

(US District Court For The District Of Colorado, CV-92-C-1781).

In these cases the banks were foreclosing on the properties using fraudulent methods such as charging exorbitant interest, illegal foreclosure, or by not crediting mortgage payments to their account, as they should have, but instead, would steal the mortgage payments for themselves, triggering foreclosure on the properties.

After running out of money they continued their fight without the help of lawyers. With some assistance by the Farmers Union a new lawsuit was filed against the Federal Lane Bank and the Farm Credit System.

The District Court ruled in their favor and ordered the banks to return the stolen properties with help from either Federal Marshals or the National Guard, but when no payments were made, the farmers declared involuntary chapter 7 bankruptcy against the Federal Land Bank and Farm Credit System.

The banks appealed their case, insisting that they were not a business but a federal agency, therefore they were not liable to pay the damages, so the farmers legal team adopted a new strategy.

According to the Federal Land Bank 1933 Charter, they are not allowed to make loans directly to applicants, but instead, could only back loans as a guarantee in case of default.

Because the Federal Land Bank had violated this rule, the farmers' legal team was able to successfully sue the bank for damages.

Word of the lawsuit began to spread. The legal team would teach others how to fight foreclosure and help them file lawsuits as well, so celebrities such as Willy Nelson joined in the case and helped raise money during his Farm Aid concerts.

Here is a short clip of Willy Nelson describing in his own words the series of events leading up to the Farmer Claims legal case.

"This whole thing started when agriculture collapsed. The housing thing came second. Gee, I've been in Farm Aid a long time, and I've been seeing farmers leave the farm. There was 8 million family farms, and now there are less than 2 million, losing 300-500 a week."

"The reason they're going is because they're going out and taking the land back, and now they're taking the houses back that they stole."

"I mean, they told the farmers to plant fence post to fence post . . . We'll take care of you, buddy . . . and loaned him more money than he could pay back, and then he winds up loosing his farm."

"Same thing happened to the house owners. Loaned him more money that he can pay back, then the next thing you know, and the government's got all the land, and all the money, and we just gave the assholes 6 or 7 more billion dollars!"

The Baskerville case had now become the Farmer Claims class action lawsuit.

Worried about the legal ramifications, the government retaliated against the farmers by hitting them with either outrageous IRS fees or by imprisoning the legal team under frivolous non-related charges. When the farmers realized they were being unfairly targeted, they and military generals, such as General Roy Schwasinger, sat in the court room to make sure that the bribed judges would vote according to constitutional law.

The farmers now with a large versus in knowledgable people filed a case to claim additional damages from the fraudulent loan activities of the Farmer Credit System.

The government tried to settle, but they had lost many cases and were now losing their appeals as well. More and more evidence was collected.

According to the National Banking Act all banks were required to register their charter with the Federal and State Bureau of Records, but none of the banks had complied, allowing the legal team to sue the Farmer Credit System.

No only was the Farmer Credit System not chartered to do business with the Banking Association, but similar American quasi government organizations such the FHA, HUD, and even the Federal Reserve Bank.

The Farmer Claims lawsuit was thrown out of court at each level, with the Records purposely destroyed, so in the early 1990's, Roy Schwasinger brought the case before the United States Supreme Court. Some of the content of this was sealed from the public eyes, but most of it can be readily seen today.

Almost unanimously the US Supreme Court Justices ruled that the Farmers Union Claims were indeed valid.

Therefore all property foreclosed by the Farmer Claims System was illegal, and those who were foreclosed on would have to receive damages.

In all, they ruled that the Federal Government and banks had defrauded the farmers *and all United States Citizens* out of vast sums of money and property.

Furthermore, the Court ruled the shocking truth that the IRS was a Puerto Rican trust, that the Federal Reserve was unlawful, that the income tax amendment was only ratified by 4 states, and therefore was not a legal amendment, and that the IRS Code was not enacted into positive law within the code of Federal Regulations, and how the federal government illegally forerclosed on farmers homes with the help from federal agencies.

Irrefutable proof was presented by a retired CIA agent. He provided testimony and records of the bank's illegal activities to leave further evidence that the Farmer Union's claims were in fact legitimate. The implications of such a decision were profound. All gold, silver and property titles taken by the Federal Reserve and the IRS must be returned to the people.

The legal team sought assistance from a small group of benevolent visionaries consisting of politicians, military generals, and business people, who had been secretly working to restore the Constitution since the 1950's. Somehow, within their ranks, a four-star Army General received high honors receiving the original 1933 US Bankruptcy proceedings. And when the case was brought before the US Supreme Court they ruled in his favor giving the Army General title over the United States, Inc.

Legal action was *then* passed on to the Senate Finance Committee and Senator Sam Nunn who was working with Roy Schwasinger.

"I will tell you the price of buying back the United States Government: it's $500 million dollars a year. In the early 90's Newt Gingrich and the republicans got together their plan, its now on the streets, its been exposed by a Columbia professor; they concluded that they could buy the United States Government for $300 million dollars a year, and by golly they did" — S. Nunn.

With the help from covert congressional and political pressure, President George Herbert Walker Bush issued an Executive Order on October 23, 1991, *Principles of Ethical Conduct for Government Officers and Employees,* which provided a provision allowing anyone who had a claim against the Federal Government to receive a payment as long as it's within the rules of the original fundamentals of the case.

According to the Federal Reserve Act of 1913, "All present and succeeding debt against the US Treasury must be assumed by the Federal Reserve." Thus the farmers' legal team was able to use that Executive Order to not only force the Federal Reserve to pay our damages in a gold backed currency but to allow them to receive legal ownership over the bankruptcy of the United States, Inc.

To collect damages, the farmers' legal team used an obscure attachment to the 14th Amendment, which most people are not aware of.

After the Civil War, the Government allowed citizens to claim a payment on anyone who suffered damages as a result of the Federal Government for failing to protect its citizens from harm of damages by a foreign government.

President Ulysses S. Grant had this attachment sealed from public eyes, but somehow someone on the farmers' legal team, got a hold of it. If you listen to that carefully, it specifies damages by a foreign government. That foreign government is the corporate Federal Government which has been masquerading to the public as the Constitutional Government.

Remember, this goes back to the organic Act of 1871 and the Trading with the Enemy Act of 1933 which defined all citizens as enemy combatants under the federal system known as THE UNITED STATES.

The Justices and farmers' legal team recognized how evil and corrupt our federal government had become and to counteract this they added some provisions in the settlement to bring the Federal Government under control.

First, they would have to be paid using a lawful currency backed by gold and silver as the Constitution dictates. This would eliminate their influence and gyrating economic cycles created by the Federal Reserve System.

Second, they would be required to go back to Common law instead of Admiralty law under the gold fringed flags. Under Common law if there is no damage done, or harm done, then there is no violation of the law. This would eliminate millions of laws which are used to control the masses and protect corrupt politicians.

Lastly, the IRS would be dismantled and replaced with a national sales tax

This is the basis of the NESARA law.

When the legal team finally settled on a figure, each individual would receive an average of $20 million dollars payout per claim. Multiplied by a total of 336,000 claims that are filed against the US Federal Government, the total payout will come out to a staggering $6.6 trillion dollars.

The US Supreme Court placed a gag-order on the case and struck all information from the Federal Registry and placed all of the records in the Supreme Court Files, up to that point.

Senator Sam Nunn kept the Baskerville Court Case within his office.

A settlement was agreed to out of court and the decision was sealed by Attorney General Janet Reno.

Because the case was sealed, claimants were not allowed to share Supreme Court Case documents with the media without violating the settlement, but they could still tell others about the lawsuit. This is probably why you haven't heard about this.

In 1991 General Roy Schwasinger went before a Senate Committee to present evidence of the bank's and the government's criminal activity. He informed them of how the corporation of the United States was tied to the establishment of the New World Order which would bring about a Fascist One Word Government ruled by the international bankers.

So in 1992, a task force was put together consisting of over 300 retired, and 35 active US Military Officers who strongly supported constitutional law.

Among them where, Admiral Jeremy M. Boorda, Chief of Naval Operations; William E. Colby, Director of the CIA, and General David J. McCloud, United States Air Force.

This Task Force was responsible for investigating government officials, Congressional officers, Judges, and the Federal Reserve.

They uncovered the common practice of bribery and extortion committed by both senators and judges.

"And every single member of Congress is impeachable for having abdicated their Article I responsibilities under the Constitution and serving as foot soldiers for the President and his mendacious Vice President."

The criminal activity was so rampant that only two out of 535 men were deemed honest, but more importantly they carried out the first ever audit of the Federal Reserve.

The Federal Reserve was used to giving out orders to politicians and had no intentions of being audited, however, after they were informed that their offices would be raided, under military gunpoint if necessary, they complied with the investigation.

After reviewing their files, the military officers found $800 trillion dollars sitting in their accounts which should have been applied to the National Debt, and contrary to federal government propaganda, they also discovered that in fact most nations owed money to the United States, instead of the other way around.

These hidden trillions were then confiscated and placed into European bank accounts in order to generate the enormous funds needed to pay the Farmer Claims class action lawsuit. Later, this money would become the basis of the Prosperity Programs.

Despite these death blows, President George H. W. Bush and the illuminati continued on with their plan of Global Enslavement.

"When we are successful, and we will be, we have a real chance at this New World Order, an Order in which a credible United Nations can use its peace keeping role to fulfill the promise and vision of the United Nations Founders." — George Bush, Sr.

In August of 1992, the military officers confronted President Bush, and demanded that he sign an agreement that he would return the United States to Constitutional Law, and ordered him to never use the term New World Order again.

Bush pretended to cooperate, but secretly planned to bring about the New World Order, anyway, by signing an Executive Order, on Dec. 25, 1992, that would have in effect closed all banks, giving Bush an excuse to declare martial law. Under the chaos of martial law, Bush intended to install a new Constitution which would have kept everyone currently in office in their same position for 25 years, and it would have removed all rights to elect new officials.

The military intervened and stopped Bush from signing that military order.

In 1993, members of the Supreme Court, certain members of Congress, and representatives from the Clinton government met with high ranking US military officers who were demanding a return to Constitutional law, reforms of the banking system and financial redress. They agreed to create the Farmer Claims Process which would allow the legal team to set up meetings all over the country on a grassroots level, to help others file claims and to educate them about the law suit.

A claim of harm can be made on any loan issued by any financial institution, for all interest paid, foreclosures, attorney and court fees, IRS taxes or liens, Real Estate and property taxes, mental and emotional stress caused by the loss of property, stress related illnesses such as suicide and divorce, and even warrants, incarceration, and probation, could also be claimed.

But the Clinton government undermined their efforts by requiring the farmer claimants to use a specific form designed by the government. This form imposed an administration fee of $300 for each claim, which was later used in 1994 as a basis to arrest the leaders of the legal team, including Roy Schwasinger. The government was so afraid of what they would say during their trial in Michigan, that extra steps were taken to conceal the true nature of the case.

County Courthouse employees were not allowed to work between Monday and Thursday during the course of the trial, and outside the Court House, FBI agents formed a perimeter preventing the media and visitors from learning what was going on, as well.

Harassment and retaliation by the government increased. Many were sent to prison, or murdered while incarcerated. Despite being protected by his military personnel, the Army General who had acquired the original 1933 title of Bankruptcy of the United States was imprisoned, killed, and replaced with a clone. This clone was then used as a decoy to prevent any further claims from being filed.

During the 1st Clinton administration, the military delayed many of Clinton's federal appointments until they were sure that these federal individuals would help restore Constitutional law. One such individual who promised to bring about the necessary changes was attorney General Janet Reno.

"If Bill and Hillary Clinton come and tell Web Hubble to tell me to do something wrong, I'm going to say, well tell him I'm not going to do it."

In agreement with the Supreme Court ruling, on June 3rd, 1993, Janet Reno ordered the Delta Force and Navy Seals to Switzerland, England, and Israel to recapture trillions of dollars of gold stolen by the Federal Reserve System from the strategic gold reserves.

These nations cooperated with the raid because they were promised their debts owed to the United States would be cancelled, and because the people who stole money from the United States also stole money from their nations as well. This bullion is to be used for the new currency backed by precious metals.

It is now safely stockpiled at the NORAD [North American Aerospace Defense command] complex in Colorado Springs, Colorado, and four other repositories.

Janet Reno's actions so enraged the powers-that-be, that it resulted in her death. She was then replaced with a clone, and with this creature who was responsible for covering up the various claim scandals. To keep the Secretary of the Treasury, Robert Rubin, in line, he too was also cloned. For their remainder in public office, both Reno and Rubin received their salaries from the International Monetary Fund [IMF], as foreign agents, and not from the US Treasury.

Despite these actions the legal team continued on with their fight while managing to avoid bloodshed and a major revolution.

After 1993, the Farmer Claims process name was changed to Bank Claims. Between 1991 and 1996 the US Supreme Court required US Citizens to file bank claims to collect damages, paid by the US Treasury Draft, This process closed in 1996.

During this time, the US Supreme Court signed one or more Justices to monitor the progress of the rulings. They enlisted the help of experts in economics, monetary systems, banking, constitutional government and law, and then in other related areas. These Justices build coalitions of support and assistance with thousands of people worldwide, know as White Knights.

The term White Knights was borrowed from the world of big business. It refers to a vulnerable company that is rescued by a corporation or a wealthy person from a hostile takeover.

To implement the required changes, the five Justices spent years negotiating how the reformations would occur. Eventually they settled on certain agreements, also known as "Accords", with the US Government, the Federal Reserve [Bank] owners, the IMF, the World Bank, and with numerous other countries, including the United Kingdom, and countries of the Euro Zone.

Because these banking reformations will impact the entire world, the IMF, World Bank, and other countries had to be involved. The reformations required that the Federal Reserve be absorbed by the US Treasury Department and the Banks' fraudulent activities must be stopped, and payment must be paid for past harm.

In 1998, the military Generals who were originally participated in the Farmer Claims process realized that the US Supreme Court Justices had no intentions of implementing the Accords, so they decided that the only way to implement the reformation was through a law passed by Congress.

In 1999, a 75 page document known as the National Economic Security and Reformations Act (NESARA) was submitted to Congress where it sat with little action for almost a year.

Late one evening, on March 9, 2000, a written quorum call was hand delivered by Delta Force and Navy Seals to 5 members of the US Senate and the US House who were sponsors and cosponsors of NESARA. They were immediately escorted by the Delta Force and Navy Seals to their respective voting chambers where they passed the National Economic Security and Reformation Act. [NESARA]

These five members of Congress were the only people who were lawfully allowed to hold office in accordance with the original 13th Amendment.

Remember, British soldiers destroyed copies of the Titles of Nobility Amendment in the War of 1812 because it prevented any one who had ties to the Crown of England from holding public office.

NESARA is the most ground-breaking Reformation to sweep, not only this country, but our planet, in its entire history. The Act does away with the Federal Reserve Bank, the IRS, the shadow government, and much, much more.

NESARA implements the following changes:
1. Zeroes out all credit card, mortgage, and other bank debt due to illegal banking and investment ac-

tivities. This is the Federal Reserve's worst nightmare, a Jubilee for Forgiveness of debt.

2. Abolishes the income tax.

3. Abolishes the IRS. Employees of the IRS will be transferred into the US Treasury National Sales Tax area.

4. Creates a 14% flat rate on non-essential "new items only" sales tax revenue for the government. In other words, food and medicine will not be taxed. Nor will used items, such as old homes.

5. Increases benefits for senior citizens.

6. Returns Constitutional Law to all courts and legal matters.

7. Reinstates the original Title of Nobility Amendment. Hundreds of thousand Americans under the control of foreign powers will lose their citizenship, be deported to other countries, and barred from re-entry for the remainder of their life. And millions of people will discover that their college degrees are now worthless paper.

8. Establishes new Presidential and Congressional elections, within 120 days after NESARA's announcement. The interim government will cancel all national emergencies and return us back to constitutional law.

9. Monitors elections and prevents illegal election activities of special interest groups.

10. Creates a new US Treasury rainbow currency backed by gold, silver, and platinum precious metals. Ending the bankruptcy of the United States initiated by Franklin Delano Roosevelt in 1933.

11. Forbids the sale of American Birth Certificate

Records as chattel property bonds, by the US Department of Transportation.

12. Initiates a new US Treasury Bank System in alignment with Constitutional Law.

13. Eliminates the Federal Reserve System. During the transition period, the Federal Reserve will be allowed to operate side by side of the US Treasury for one year, in order to remove all Federal Reserve Notes from the money supply.

14. Restores financial privacy.

15. Retrains all judges and attorneys in Constitutional Law.

16. Ceases all aggressive US Government military actions world wide.

17. Establishes peace throughout the world.

18. Releases enormous sums of money for humanitarian purposes.

19. Enables the release of over 6,000 patents of suppressed technologies that are being withheld from the public, under the guise of national security, including free energy devises, antigravity and sonic healing machines.

"I want the American people to know today that I am still committed to working with people of good faith and good will of both parties to do what's best for our country." — President William Clinton.

Because President Clinton's clone had no interest in signing NESARA into law, on October 10, 2000, under orders from the US Military Generals, the elite Naval Seals and Delta Force stormed the White House and then, at gunpoint, forced Bill Clinton to sign NESARA into law.

During this time the Secret Service and the White House security personnel were ordered to stand down and were disarmed, and allowed to witness this event under a gag order.

From its very inception, Bush, Sr., the Corporate government, major bank houses, and the Carlyle Group have opposed NESARA.

To maintain secrecy the case details and the docket number were sealed and revised within the official Congressional Registry to reflect a commemorative coin, and then, again, it was revised even more recently. This is why there are no public Congressional records, and why a search for this law will not yield the correct details, until after the Reformations are made public.

You probably never heard of this law due to an extremely strict gag order placed upon politicians, media personnel, and bank officers.

Even though Alex Jones or Ron Paul will not tell you about it, the law is still valid, and members of Congress will not tell us any of this, because they have been ordered by the Supreme Court Justices to deny the existence of NESARA or face charges of treason punishable by death.

Some members of Congress have been actually charged with obstruction of justice.

"We're here to the nation's capital to tell the story that we've got an economic convulsion in agriculture; we've got a lot of broken dreams, a lot of broken families, a lot of broken lives, and we're not going to take it an longer."

Minnesota Senator Paul Wellstone was about to break the gag order, but before he could, his small passenger plane crashed killing his wife, daughter, and himself. If this isn't enough to keep Congress in line, money is. The CIA routinely bribes Senators with stolen loot from the Bank Roll programs. Every Senator has been bribed with a minimum of $200 million dollars deposited into a Bank of America account in Canada.

You will never hear the media networks report about NESARA. To maintain silence, major news networks, such as CNN, are paid to the tune of $2 billions dollars annually.

Some of this loot is funneled by the Mormon Church in Utah through Senator Orrin Hatch's office and Bank of America.

Not only is Congress bribed, but the entire Joint Chiefs of Staff, and the upper tier of the government, including the President himself, receive these payments as well. Only the Provost Marshal has the lawful authority to arrest these individuals, but sadly, he won't do his job either. It seems the United States Military is full of pencil pushing politicians who care more about advancement than doing their jobs, and not surprisingly, much dis-information about NESARA can be found on the Internet.

Prominent naysayers include *quartloos.com* which is rumored to be a CIA front; *nesara.org,* which is maintained by the Bush family; Sherry Shiner and various internet channelers, receiving their messages from psychopathic spooks, have all contributed to the confusion.

Even the information of Wikipedia is in error. Wikipedia gives you the history of CIA agent Harvey Barnard's NESARA law. If you look closely, this law stands for the **National Economic Stabilization and Recovery Act** which would have made reforms to the economy to replace the Income Tax with a national sales tax. This law was rejected by Congress in the 1990's. But there is little mention of the **National Economic Security and Reformation Act** on Wikipedia, or its ramifications.

The next step is to announce NESARA to the world, but its not an easy task to do. Many powerful groups have tried to prevent the implementation of NESARA.

The NESARA Law requires that at least once a year an effort be made to announce the law to the public. Three current US Supreme Court Judges control the committee in charge of NESARA's announcement. These judges have used their overall authority to seek to sabotage its announcement.

In 2001, after much negotiation, the Supreme Court Justices ordered the current Congress to pass resolutions approving NESARA. This took place on September 9, 2001, 18 months after NESARA become law. On September 10, 2001, George Bush Sr. moved into the White House to steer his son on how to block the announcement.

The next day, on September 11, 2001, at 10:00 AM, EDT, Allan Greenspan was scheduled to announce the new US Treasury Bank System, debt forgiveness for all US Citizens, and the abolishment of the IRS, as a first part of the public announcement of NESARA.

Just before the announcement, at 9:00 AM, Bush Sr. ordered the demolition of the World Trade Center, to stop the international banking computers on floors one and two, in the North Tower, from initiating a new US Treasury Bank System.

Explosives in the World Trade Center were planted by the CIA, and Mossad operatives, and detonated remotely in building 7, which was demolished later that day, in order to cover up their crime.

Remote pilot technology was used in a fly-over event to deliver a payload of explosives into the Pentagon, at the exact location of the White Knights, at their new Naval Command Center, who were coordinating activity supporting NESARA's implementation, nationwide.

With the announcement of NESARA stopped dead in its tracks, George Bush Sr. decapitated any hopes of returning the government back to the people.

While CIA agent, Osama Ben Laden, is made into the boogy man, the country dashed off to fight a war on terror.

The events of 911 eventually led the way to the slaughter of the Iraqi people. To keep the public unaware of the carnage, the official death count of US soldiers and Iraqi civilians is purposely under reported.

Deceased US soldiers are either being dumped into the Persian Gulf, or replaced with clones. As of 2009 the total death count of Iraqi civilians now surpasses a staggering 1.6 million people!

The same cooked statistics apply to the death totals on the day of 911. According to the government, 2,752 people died that day, when in actuality, 30,700 people had died.

No one questions the insanely small numbers given out by the government, because New York City is a large place. People with lost loved ones do not make contact with others, so they have no way of knowing actually how many people have died.

WAR ON TERROR CASUALTIES REPORT
[Not For Public Release]
DOD ID: 179BR82
Office of the Chairman
The Joint Chiefs of Staff
Washington, DC 20319-9999

The Bush family was originally offered $300 trillion dollars to cooperate with NESARA but instead they chose to maintain their control over us; so in the end, the Bush family will end up with nothing.

The Attacks of 911 had managed to stop the announcement of NESARA dead in its tracks. Many more attempts have been made over the years but the Bush family has managed to stop them.

These people won't be able to get away with their crimes forever. Little by little their wealth is being dismantled right before their eyes.

Before NESARA is announced to the public it was stipulated that the original Farmer Claims, first be paid out, with a bullion backed currency issued by the US Treasury. In other words, they cannot be paid in Federal Reserve Notes.

The $6.6 trillion dollar Farmer Claims payout is to be distributed in the form of ATM Debit Cards. Remember, this money will come from the Bank Rolls and Prosperity Programs. The only catch is that to distribute these funds they must first be released by the trustees whose members come from the Clinton, Bush, and Rockefeller families.

They are doing everything they possibly can to stop these payouts.

One way is to transport the banking documents, which contain instructions on how to access these funds, in a never ending loop, 24/7, between warehouses in Charlotte North Carolina, and Washington DC. The drivers of these Fed Ex Trucks are heavily bribed, and many of them are afraid of being arrested by the Department of Homeland Security if they were actually to deliver their payload, as required by law.

At one point, after the packages were returned to Washington DC, President George W. Bush placed them under military quard. Federal Judges ordered him to release the funds, but Bush [the younger], replied, *"You will never receive these packages, they belong to me."*

The judge answered, *"I can do no more; he is the President of the United States."* The only option left is to arrest the President, but the police commissioner, the Provost Marshal, and the military, refuse to help.

This cycle has been ongoing for years. The only alternative left is to kill the Federal Reserve System by force. The problem is that George Bush, and now Obama, have threatened to use the dollar as a weapon of mass destruction against the nations of the world, to comply with the New Word Order agenda.

Bush once commented, *"The people will now suffer greatly."*

The world cannot tolerate this. The dollar must be removed as the international world's currency, and replaced with a new independent assets based monetary unit backed by precious metals.

On December 15, 2006, a meeting was arranged to discuss ways to curtail these criminal activities. Their ranks included representatives from the global family who were enlightened individuals working directly under Saint Germain. They include members from the IMF, the World Bank, the Rothschild family, and key persons from over 48 nations.

They agreed to implement *three goals* by June 15, 2007, that is [1] to end all war, [2] to actively improve the environment, and [3] to actively provide abundance for their people.

Those nations which will not keep this agreement will eventually be cut off from the international banking community in order to force them into compliance.

On September 19, 2007, a new global banking system was approved by Congress.

On October 19, 2007, at midnight, the US Treasury of the Republic went on line with a new gold backed banking system, but this gold banking system is not being deployed, because the banks are trying to dispose of their worthless derivatives before they get set to zero, when the new gold backed currency valuations go into force.

To improve the stability of the banking system, in

1988 the BIS implemented Basel I, which required banks to hold 6% net capital. On December 1st, 2007, this went a step further, when Basel II was implemented, requiring all loans to be backed by the appropriate collateral, and raise net capital requirements to 8%.

The new rules prevent the bankers from collateralizing their derivatives with stolen money from collateral accounts and Prosperity funds. Furthermore, all assets must be valued according to the daily market price, also know as the "market to market" rule.

Any bank which refuses to comply with Basel II will be cut off from international markets, which is why American banks demanded $700 billion dollars from the *Troubled Asset Relief Program.* If they didn't get this bailout, the banks would have shut their doors, inciting Marshal Law.

On June 15, 2009, Basel III was initiated which goes a step further than Basel II, by requiring the banks to disclose any previously undisclosed junk assets, or derivatives marked off the balance sheet.

Jack Blog has investigated financial fraud for the federal government, for over 30 years. He has found that the banks use off balance sheet financial operations to hide money in places like the Caymen Islands.

"If a bank, for example, has done bad lending, they put it in a portfolio of an offshore entity. No one will be able to figure out what that offshore entity is worth, and its that kind of transaction that has actually disabled the world financial system. I think every bank at this point should be forced to come absolutely clean about how much money it has in these offshore shells, of different kinds, and how many deals more are hidden in the balance sheets and on the books."

Under Basel III, every bank transaction must be disclosed on the balance sheet. But if this were to happen, these banks would become insolvent over night, and would not be able to pass their fake stress test.

The Federal Reserve System is fighting tooth and nail to prevent this disclosure, because if their $500 trillion dollars or so of derivatives were actually placed on their balance sheet, using the "market to market" rule, they would be shown to be bankrupt.

Some banks are now working to bring about the NESARA mission in hopes that the Prosperity funds would trickle into their banks, saving them from closing their doors, but most of the larger banks that are fighting the coming changes will soon be out of business. They are not informing their employees of the new regulation and thus will not be ready to operate under a gold banking charter.

Slowly, the illegal practices of the international financiers are coming to an end. One by one the mayor banking houses are imploding right before our eyes.

Their train wreck is occurring because these banks are no longer allowed to use assets from the collateral account of the global debt Facility to backup their loans. This is why we are seeing their derivatives implode.

The banks have been illegally using the collateral account, as collateral for their gold backed derivatives, bullion certificates, and bonds sold to offshore domiciled corporations.

With the new Basel II rules in place these derivative assets have now become worthless garbage, resulting in the massive banking writ-downs you see today.

According to the *Office of International Treasury Control* this over-the-counter derivative market is worth about $3.3 quadrillion dollars; with J.P. Morgan leading the pack, with hundreds of trillion dollars of derivatives.

During the Clinton years, the banking 1:10 fractional reserve ratio was increased to 1:100. This easy money allowed anyone to get a home loan resulting in the housing sector boom.

Since many of these loans were made to risky low income households, the banks deferred their risk by selling their loan portfolios to investors, in a process known as Securitization. This occurs when mortgages are repackaged with other mortgages in a giant pool of liquidity, which are sold to investors on the global market.

These credit derivatives can then be repackaged and leveraged again at another 100:1 ratio, which is then repeated, over and over, until there is literally quadrillions of dollars of derivatives floating around in the world's bankrupt system.

When housing prices were going up, these derivatives were making fortunes for the banks' and the government's offshore accounts, allowing them to buy up assets all over the world with virtually free money.

When investors realized these derivatives contained toxic loans, they stopped their buying binge causing the credit market to seize up, which is why housing prices are in free fall.

Because no one wants to buy these toxic derivatives, the banks and the government are now in a panic to find other people's money to plug up the holes in the cracking dam.

Though some funds have been raised by selling military secrets to China, or through CIA drug running operations, this is nowhere near enough money to prop up a collapsing derivative market; so now the government is resorting to stealing the money, which is no credible way to run a country.

To put a stop to this criminal activity, in December, 2009, INTERPOL was given legal jurisdiction within the US, to hunt down and arrest crooked bankers.

April 4, 2008 marked the expiration of the 70 year bankruptcy agreement of the United States, beginning in 1938. Technically, the Bankruptcy began in 1933, but the Supreme Court did not enforce it until the United States became a legislative democracy in 1938.

The nations of the world, weary of the shenanigans of the Federal Reserve System, knew they had a limited time to foreclose on the United States before the corporate government could extend another 70 year extension of the Bankruptcy.

Without this protection, the government was now at the mercy of its creditors who were demanding reforms of the banking system, such as higher net capital requirements found under Basel II. If the United States failed to meet their demands, they would be cut off from the international markets.

So to raise the funds needed, in August, 2008, the US Government began shorting the derivative market causing stock and commodity prices to fall worldwide. But this $20 trillion dollars of wealth was not destroyed; instead, it was transferred into the government's offshore pension fund accounts, of which $5 trillion dollars were moved back into the United States, to shore up a collapsing dollar.

Soon, this money will run out, leaving the option of either crashing the financial market, or once again destroying what little is left of our American economy, or by printing more money, leading to hyperinflation.

But the global family does not want to see a devaluated dollar, as 90% of all US dollars in circulation today   are held by foreigners; and they have no desire to see their assets evaporate, so they have agreed to back all dollars, printed before September 2008, with gold stored in the Philippines; at the rate of 1.28 grams of gold per dollar.

This would serve to curb the inflationary activities of the Federal Reserve, and the assets of the hard working average American, but on the other hand, all derivatives would be valued at 1/3rd of 1%, which is their fair market value, forcing those who own this toxic trash into bankruptcy and finally out of business.

On September 30th, 2009, the fiscal year of the United States came to a close. Because of the precarious financial situation of the United States, and its derivative holdings, the Chinese government reversed its policy of accepting fiat money for repayment of the national debt, so instead, they will only accept gold and silver as lawful payment, as specified in Article 1, Section 10 of the United States Constitution.

To meet these new demands, the owners of the Federal Reserve System are scrambling to purchase enough gold and silver; but no one wants to sell them any.

While the Federal Reserve System is falling apart, Barry Sotero continues to block the NESARA deliveries. Even though he never invested any money in these programs, he demands a portion of these funds for himself.

In a pattern which mimics the Bush years, the Obama administration continues to make new daily attempts to steal the funds. But before he was even sworn into office, in December, 2008, Obama tried unsuccessfully to steal $400 billion dollars from the Prosperity funds, and demanded another $1 trillion dollars ransom for his deed.

A week before his inauguration, Saint Germain and the global family had confronted Obama about his actions. At that time, Obama agreed to go along with the NESARA mission, but soon after reversed his promise and has now solidified his alliance with the Bush/Clinton cabal.

http://www.myspace.com/68129957/classic

Continuing

Prosperity Programs & NESARA

Since the beginning of our known recorded history humans have used barter and exchange in society.

Since the earliest days of time, people have used items of value as a barter tool for goods and services.

The Money Changers have always sought to control the exchange system as one method of the enslavement of man. Take for example the story of Jesus driving the Money Changers out of the temple. The Money Changers required worshipers to exchange their gifts (of spices, wares and precious metals etc.) into a specific form of currency (the temple tax) for a fee.

Over the ages the Money Changers have been hard at work controlling the barter, or currency system that we know today as money.

The Money Changers have been working most diligently at perfecting the money changer concept. Today we know it as fractional reserve banking. To put it simply, based on a $1000 value of gold they issue $10,000 (or more) paper dollars or pounds. (for a ratio of 10 or even much more to 1).

The Money Changers charge the issuing government interest on every dollar or pound printed or created by effortless key strokes on a computer.

The current monetary system is the Money Changers on steroids! The primary examples of the fractional reserve predator's are The Bank of England and The Federal Reserve. These institutions are controlled not by the government, but by individuals, or the Money Changers themselves.

You are encouraged to learn more about this system of enslavement in order to prevent it from happening again.

Part of The Plan by the forces of Redemption is to break up this monopoly game of control. This is happening before your very eyes. The financial tsunami you are witnessing is the Money Changers' enslavement system collapsing under it's own weight. The system has become so corrupt it is unable to withstand the light of day.

Basel II and III banking protocols are being instituted which force the banks and financial institutions to open their crooked books to the light. The result is what you can read about in your news sources today — total bank failure. This is part of a grand design to release humanity from the strangle hold of a corrupt financial system designed to maintain total control. Just ponder for a moment on how money and the current form of barter affects every aspect of your life!

There are many elements to The Plan. One of those elements is NESARA and The Prosperity Programs.

The monetary Trust Fund of St. Germain was established in the 18th century. This trust fund was based upon precious metals and minerals (gold, silver, diamonds etc.). Because the funds were based upon these constant items of value, they were immune to the control of currency systems of the money changers of the day. The values of gold and precious minerals have only increased and recently have begun to sky rocket. Look at the value of gold today against the currency systems. There are also massive reserves of precious metals and minerals hidden away from the money changers in our Mother Earth. NESARA is the **National Economic Security and Reformation Act.**

The NESARA Act is actually part of a global plan. It is designed to dismantle the United States financial system that controls the de facto standard currency of the whole world.

When NESARA is announced and implemented the Prosperity Programs, Farm Claims, and other trusts will also be released.

The recipients include individuals and governments. Most of the recipients are unknown, as a form of protection from the Elite. The overall plan has been kept secret, as you will learn in your own research. This has been and continues to be a strategic element of the plan.

The Money Changers have been hard at work in preventing the enactment of the plan, as you will learn. When the funds are distributed some of the recipients will be required to disburse a certain percentage of their funds to others. They will be required to locate suitable persons that are willing to use the funds for the LOVE of mankind.

Eventually every man woman and child on Earth will benefit from the programs. The idea is to flood the world with so much prosperity that the pursuit of happiness will become the only goal for all mankind. Governments and individuals will no longer be able to use currency to control humanity.

Right now Patriot Workers are being encouraged to become involved and use their gifts to facilitate this Republic plan. We are being encouraged to use the Love and Light within us to come up with personal and government projects to insure the use of funds for the good of all mankind.

You are being asked to conceive of projects that you feel are worthy pursuits to help and educate all the people of the world. To help to restore the beauty and magnificence of the world. If you had unlimited resources what would you do?

You have been prepared for this mission, now is the time to get busy and make it happen. You are encouraged to ask for guidance, use your personal interests and skills to develop projects to help bring all of mankind into the Light. We have been told over and over that God is NOT going to do this FOR us.

There is not going to be a magical solution to all of the worlds problems. **We are the warriors of Light and Love! Now is the time to get to work.** Think about it. How did you think we were going to make a difference? This is but one part of the overall plan.

The elements of Love and Light are with you, encouraging you every step of the way. Listen to your heart and it will guide you upon your path. You will instinctively know what to do at the right time.

The collapse of the Dark Cabal is imminent! Your time to really shine has come.

1
Confirmation

Neil Keenan and Keith Scott to Benjamin Fulford

This letter came in and confirms what I have been hearing from my sources in Europe, Japan and the US. We are near the end game. Humanity is about to be freed.

Dear Benjamin,

It is all coming down : —

The meeting between the 57 Finance Ministers from around the world that took place on board a ship off the coast of Monaco is beginning to quietly emerge as a powerful and dynamic shift in Global Economics and potentially in Global Politics as former Presidents and Prime Ministers of countries who have sided with the Banking Cabal, are now already jumping ship and supporting the growing movement toward proper financial management of the Global Accounts around the World.

A cataclysmic shift in both Global Politics and Economics is now well under way. World Governments are coming to understand how the Global Banking System is systematically looting entire economies through theft, fraud, deception and manipulation, which in turn forces Governments to raise taxes that citizens should not have to pay.

At the meeting of 57 an understanding was created and this understanding has been formalized by the Co-Hosts of that meeting, the Swiss Government. Our internal information indicates more than 80 Governments have issued the Acknowledgement of Memorandum of the Agreement and will formally sign when all Governments who have been invited to sign, formally do so. Also from internal sources, we know that many more Governments will sign. Governments are starting to wise up to what are the underlying causes of financial disaster around the World. Their response is simple and if it could be paraphrased it would be "It is time to get these bums who think they run the world from behind closed doors, and drown them like the rats they are".

This now means that those, who in their arrogance sought to dominate and control the masses through their subterfuge and fraud, have deluded themselves into a corner from where there is now no escape for them. The entire financial mess the world is in will now prove to be a mirage that we, the innocent taxpayer, have been led to believe in. Banks will soon be forced to abide by their Charters and to undertake business strictly according to their Charters. The days of moving public income to the private side ledgers of the banks while they move their private liabilities to the public side ledgers are almost over.

The Banks have blamed the public for overspending. Yet when the economy was hit in 2008 and there was need to provide the TARP funds to keep banks solvent, the banking gurus decided the citizens needed to spend more to kick start the economy. Then the Banks blame all the problems on the taxpayer, when in truth it was the Banks who were stealing and gambling with funds they mirrored from the Global Accounts for underwriting purposes. In fact, they actually called the Global Account bonds as "Casino Bonds". I can bet, Heads I win and Tails, I don't lose…the collateral accounts do. Great deal.

The whole thing was started when white dragon society members had 134.5 Billion in bearer bonds stolen from them by Daniele dal Bosco and a renegade officer of the now defunct Office of International Treasury Control (OITC), David Sale. Sale, who despised his former boss Ray C. Dam deliberately set about to malign Ray C Dam and another former officer of OITC, a White Dragon, to Cambodian press and on various internet sites and Sale eventually sent documents he forged to Cambodian Police with the intention of incriminating Ray C. Dam and the White Dragon. Sale believed he could take over OITC by conspiring with Giancarlo Bruno and others from the World Economic Forum, who in turn conspired to embroil and indeed did involve Ban Ki Moon, the Secretary General of the United Nations, in the illegal use of Bonds stolen from the White Dragons.

We have a world where the conveniences of power, money and deceit transform into levels of corruption, fraud and theft that stagger the mind with their proportions. We have people who see what is right and needs to be done, being ambushed by situations that destroy them as being useful in fighting the cabal that has threatened to enslave the world.

What nobody realized would happen, did happen.

When the OITC member became friends with the White Dragon Society, not enemies, that friendship was based on doing what is right and best for the world even in the face of the darkest and most blatant threats against their lives. A gunfight took place near the White Dragon member's home between those who would eliminate him and those who have been sent there to protect him. A known mafioso was caught near the home of a another White Dragon in Switzerland who had been helping. Sale made attempts to hire people in Italy to eliminate yet another White Dragon. Recently he had a very narrow escape when three heavy bags dropped from possibly as high as 35 floors above missed him by mere inches. Ray C. Dam was imprisoned for more than eight months in Cambodia and we know people were paid to dispose of him permanently an activity that it seems the Government of Cambodia tolerated and the United States Government refused to render any assistance to Dam, a United States citizen. He only survived due to the efforts of the White Dragon Society members. These men know the dangers, as key people who were close to them have been eliminated in the past. A White Dragon friend Joe Bendana died in very suspicious circumstances in New Jersey. Another friend was lost in Andreas Jawurek, a Swiss lawyer who pushed the envelope too far with one of the banks and who was found with a gunshot wound to the head.

White Dragon Society members presented the plans they developed and their intentions to the Governments who attended the meeting in Monaco and the Governments like it. One key White Dragon may have his enemies, but he has emerged from over 20 years of working around the Global Accounts to become one of the very few in the world with a true understanding of economics as they relate to these accounts. Another one is a pit bull that knows no fear and has the clarity of mind and purpose that staggers the imagination.

The plan calls for a complete reigning in of the banks and to force them to work according to their Charters, and bankers who fail to comply will face the consequences of their actions. In America, it has been estimated that the US Debt could be eliminated with less than four years through this one device. Taxes could be driven down to their lowest level since the beginning of the nineteenth century.

It is estimated that taxes on the people could be reduced heavily and in many cases eliminated. This is done simply by forcing Banks to pay back to Treasury what they have been stealing in almost every country in the World. Force them to make proper pass back to Treasury Direct instead of stealing the wealth of their clients through fraud and deception.

Put this together with proper oversight, which will take men of resolve and courage such as the above mentioned White Dragons, men who understand the real cause of economic problems, and then the economic problems we are told exist, will simply vanish, for they are no more than a mirage. If you do not believe this, then add the trillions in profits that banks tender as trading profits and the bonuses they pay themselves for the United States alone, and you will have considerably more than the annual deficit growth. Are these earnings from honest labor? Not at all. They are the earnings gained from misrepresentation, fraud, theft, deception and manipulation. The steal the homes of hard working people, people who have been disadvantaged by the rush of banks to pay shareholders ever increasing dividends and themselves ever increasing salaries and bonuses.

Clean up the trading markets of banks and ensure money goes where it is supposed to go.

Once the accounts are in the hands of men who will ensure they are used as they should be, then the problems the world faces today in the disenfranchisement of the working middle class will cease. All countries will have equitable access to the Global Accounts, no matter what their politics.

This change is coming. The countries that have already decided their assets within the Global Accounts System shall be brought under proper control have also decided that Keenan and Scott, the men who have defined where the problems really lie and have fearlessly moved to resolve these problems should also be the men who will oversee the accounts.

We are on the cusp of a whole new era for the world.

One thing the "rats" should realize, no matter how powerful they think they are, Governments make the laws. In the end, these rats that own the Federal Reserve System and the Global Banking System are subject to law, and their days manipulating politicians will come to a very hard end as the politicians wake up.

Blessings,

Senior International Finance official.

NESARA II

2
The Monaco Colloquium

August 2011. The Great Game approaches its final shake of the dice. Switzerland leads a fifty-seven nation geopolitical board change. The current governments of the US, Canada, UK, Germany, France and Italy are actively excluded from executive decisions concerning the new global gold-backed financial system.

It was a step-change moment destined to be savored by future historians. For the period of a week towards the end of August 2011, a secret meeting of fifty-seven finance ministers from across the globe began the long-prepared-for task of setting up a new international asset-backed financial system.

The gathering was a powerful invitation-only colloquium, hosted by Switzerland, which started on dry land in the Principality of Monaco & Monte-Carlo, and then moved onto a major naval vessel in adjacent international waters. In subsequent commentary, this conference has sometimes been referred to as "The Meeting of 57". (Chapter 2)

Nations represented at the meeting in an official government capacity included Switzerland, The Netherlands, Czechoslovakia, Bulgaria, Romania, China, Russia, Brazil, Argentina, Uruguay, Paraguay, Venezuela and several Gulf Cooperation Council states. Canada was represented in a non-governmental capacity. Various positive transnational power groupings were also present, such as the White Dragon Society (Chapter 3) and the US Pentagon-CIA-NSA reform faction (Chapter 2).

Certain negative fiat-casino players were strenuously refused entry. These included the recently deposed Japanese Prime Minister, Naoto Kan, the Managing Director of the IMF, Christine Lagarde, and all members of the US Nazi-continuum (the Rockefeller-Kissinger-Bush syndicate).

For Jay Rockefeller it was like being thrown out of his own funeral. Having last year lost Europe to the Rothschilds, and more recently lost Japan to the White Dragon Society, he was now physically and forcibly removed from the Monaco Colloquium by agents acting for the US Pentagon White Hats.

Initially resorting to patrician Illuminati bluster, Rockefeller attempted to talk his way into the Monaco meeting. He was rebuffed. "Do you know who I am?" he demanded. "Yes, I know who you are. You are nobody," said the host's man at the door. "The Old World Order is out and a New World Order is about to begin." Rockefeller raged to no effect and was informed that this was now a brave new world for the young; old mummies like him were merely dust to be swept away.

Jay Rockefeller left the entrance, collected a security detail of BlackOps goons, and returned in an attempt to force entry. The Monaco Colloquium summoned its own security and, according to eye-witness reports, Rockefeller and his cowboys were "literally thrown out."

Shortly afterwards, the land-based part of the meeting was adjourned, the attendees boarded a large naval vessel and continued their conference in international waters off the coast. Two of Rockefeller's BlackOps helicopters buzzed the boat, intent, it is said, on activating listening technology and using electro-magnetic pulse weapons (http://tinyurl.com/6j54r6o) to disrupt proceedings. If this is true as reported, the importance of the meeting would be difficult to over-estimate. Within moments of the choppers' appearance, US military aircraft, described as Harrier jump jets, arrived and forced the helicopters away.

The opposition of two openly conflicting and powerful US interest groups (Rockefeller syndicate vs Pentagon White Hats) raises an important, if covert, operational issue. Which faction now controls the clone-labs at Camp David (Maryland) and elsewhere? Whose finger can switch off the sleeper cells? Which prominent clone-lines might be terminated first? This is a large and emerging topic of current concern.

Another important side-issue arising from the active participation of several South American reformist governments at the Monaco Colloquium, was the confiscation of the Nazi-continuum's bank assets, BlackOps bases and residential boltholes scattered all over the continent. These have been multiplied and much-developed since the Nazi diaspora first established itself in South America in the immediate aftermath of the Second World War.

One of the facilities under immediate threat of confiscation is said to be the Bush family hideaway in Paraguay. In the autumn of 2006, George Bush Snr purchased a one hundred thousand acre ranching estate outside Paso de Patria, in the Ñeembucú department of Paraguay.

The property is strategically located over the Guarani aquifer. (http://tinyurl.com/6zj8od3) The Bush family first got to know about the ranch through their CIA-linked drug-running activities in the area in the nineteen eighties and nineties. Located near the border with Brazil and Bolivia, the estate offers a range of covert entry and escape routes. Private meetings and arrangements with Paraguay's then-president, Nicanor Duarte, indicated that there would be no political difficulties with the Bush residence and its security.

However, by April 2008, the political situation in Paraguay was beginning to volatilise after decades of dictatorial stability. The Patriotic Front for Change coalition was on the move. Fernando Lugo, a bearded, left-lean-

ing, dissentient Roman Catholic ex-bishop won Paraguay's Presidential election on the 20th April 2008, decisively upsetting the sixty-year human rights horror-rule of the right wing Colorado Party.

Lugo had been actively opposed by the Vatican, ostensibly because of his enthusiasm for Liberation Theology and its spiritual objective of subverting the Paraguayan élite status quo. He was also a powerful and popular advocate of land reforms.

In Paraguay, less than two per cent of the population owns more than ninety per cent of the land, and forty per cent of the population lives in poverty. "We have 300,000 families without land and they have the constitutional right to own the soil they live on," Lugo insists. If the Bush family had made private and personal arrangements with Nicanor Duarte, it is thought unlikely that Fernando Lugo and his government, emboldened by the revolutionary news out of Monaco, will continue to honour them for much longer.

The introduction of a new pan-global asset-backed financial system to replace the fiat-paper casino now visibly collapsing in the West has been a long-anticipated reform. That it is now coming to political focus at so many national levels outside the Western Cabal is only to be expected. As the ever-increasing debt-pressures impact on food and energy prices, and on employment opportunities worldwide, political instability is becoming pandemic.

The Monaco Colloquium kickstarted the only financial solution which can solve the problem. What was discussed there connects closely with Global Debt Forgiveness (Chapter 4), with overcoming the Washington DC corporation's blocking of the disbursement of the $47 trillion World Global Settlement Funds, (Chapter 5), with the implementation of the $10 trillion US Dollar Refunding Project, and with the return to an internationally-accepted Gold Standard.

At The Monaco Colloquium an understanding was created and formalised by the co-hosts of that meeting, the Swiss Government. By the second week of September 2011, more than eighty sovereign national governments across the world had issued the Acknowledgement of Memorandum of the Agreement, and had undertaken to formally sign the document at the pre-agreed moment. Many more than this core eighty group of nations are expected to commit to, and enact, the Agreement.

Among other things, the Monaco initiative will abolish the US Federal Reserve Board, delegitimise and ban all fiat paper currencies from international circulation and trading, and introduce several new gold-backed international currencies, some with completely new names.

NESARA II

3
The Meeting Of 57

<u>August 30, 2011</u>. Benjamin Fulford, "Secret meeting of 57 finance ministers on ship charts new financial system"…"Humanity will be set free soon"

Re: August 29, 2011 — The last six words sum this one up nicely. *"Humanity will be set free soon."*

This report describes more details of the demise of the "world dark cabal", or as it was called last week, *"the world military industrial pharmaceutical medical banking congressional corporate educational religious nutty nougat caramel complex."* Overall a very promising report from Ben.

Highlights

• …a secret meeting of 57 finance ministers aimed at setting up a new international financial system took place in a large ship on international waters near Europe … deliberately excluded [were] representatives from the US Federal Reserve Board and its Washington D.C. subsidiary, France, Italy, the UK, Germany and Japan.

• A foundation will be set up as a vehicle to finance the military industrial complex to ensure payrolls continue to be met at the agencies and the pentagon during the transition to a constitutional government in the United States

• US and European elements of the White Dragon Society will be preparing legal cases to ensure the arrest of all leading conspirators in their plan to murder over 85% of the world's population.

• ...if the seismographic graph of the so-called earthquake that hit Washington D.C. last week is not a fake, then it appears that indeed a nuclear weapon was detonated at or near a known underground facility.

• ...several South American government representatives at the 57 country meeting on the ship promised to start confiscating refuge land bought by the genocidal faction in countries like Uruguay, Paraguay and Argentina.

• In Japan, meanwhile, a new Prime Minister has been selected who appears to be outside of the control of the Zionist cabal. Yoshihiko Noda, ... Rockefeller tainted candidates... were...excluded.

• The White Dragon Society will be calling on Japanese underground and right wing figures this week to demand that they now cease all cooperation with the genocidal Zionist faction.

• *"Humanity will be set free soon.*

Secret meeting of 57 finance ministers on ship charts new financial system

Benjamin Fulford, August 30, 2011

For the past week, a secret meeting of 57 finance ministers aimed at setting up a new international financial system took place in a large ship on international waters near Europe, according to White Dragon Society representatives who were there. The meeting, hosted by Switzerland, deliberately excluded representatives from the US Federal Reserve Board and its Washington D.C. subsidiary; France; Italy; the UK; Germany;and Japan. Countries like Russia, China and the Netherlands were among the 57 represented.

Representatives from the Pentagon and the US agencies at the meeting promised to bypass the Federal Reserve board and use their access to codes for the international collateral accounts to finance the US military industrial complex in conjunction with the new system.

The Swiss used their financial intelligence to refuse would-be participants who were in any way associated with either the Bilderberg Group, the Council on Foreign Relations or the Trilateral Commission. Among those refused entry were Naoto Kan (still Prime Minister of Japan as of last week), IMF head Christine Lagarde and US Senator J. Rockefeller. Rockefeller was actually physically prevented from boarding the ship, according to two eye-witnesses.

There was an attempt by members of the old world order fascist cabal to eavesdrop on the meeting with helicopters. The helicopters were also preparing to attack the ship with pulse weapons before they were warned off by pentagon white hats and forced to leave the vicinity, CIA sources say.

A foundation will be set up as a vehicle to finance

the military industrial complex to ensure payrolls continue to be met at the agencies and the pentagon during the transition to a constitutional government in the United States, the sources said. The foundation will, as a temporary security measure for security reasons, exclude all members of the Khazarian, Sabbatean sect, including as well, any US/Israeli dual citizens.

US and European elements of the White Dragon Society will be preparing legal cases to ensure the arrest of all leading conspirators in their plan to murder over 85% of the world's population. Videos of 5 separate underground cities, complete with agricultural complexes, were shown to meeting participants as evidence of the genocide planned for 2012.

In a related development, multiple sources claim two of the underground cities, one near Washington D.C. and another near Denver, Colorado, were destroyed by nuclear weapons last week. Some sources, also connected to intelligence circles, however, deny that such an attack took place.

Nevertheless, if the seismographic graph of the so-called earthquake that hit Washington D.C. last week is not a fake, then it appears that indeed a nuclear weapon was detonated at or near a known underground facility. Instead of showing a series of small quakes building up into a huge one as seen in natural quakes, the graph shows a sudden huge shake followed by smaller after-shocks typical of an explosion.

The message to the cabalists seems to be simple: "you will not be given access to your underground shelters while the rest of us die."

It is also interesting to note that several South American government representatives at the 57 country meeting on the ship promised to start confiscating refuge land bought by the genocidal faction in countries like Uruguay, Paraguay and Argentina. This will mean, for example, the Bush ranch in Paraguay will be seized soon.

In Japan, meanwhile, a new Prime Minister has been selected who appears to be outside of the control of the Zionist cabal. Yoshihiko Noda, is a graduate of the Matsushita academy, who represents a moderate, nationalist and pro-business element of the Japanese establishment. More importantly, Rockefeller tainted candidates linked to ex-power broker Ozawa, such as Banri Kaeida and Zionist pet Seiji Maehara, were both excluded.

There will be a major push over the coming weeks to start purging Zionist slaves from the Japanese political, military and bureaucratic establishment. The purge will be concentrated on only a few key high level traitors. Most importantly, since former Prime Minister Junichiro Koizumi has run off to North Korea, it is now the turn for former Prime Minister Yasuhiro Nakasone and his fellow Rockefeller stooges to surrender.

The White Dragon Society will be calling on Japanese underground and right wing figures this week to demand that they now cease all cooperation with the genocidal Zionist faction. They will be excluded from the new financial system if they do not agree. The White Dragon allies are willing and able to go to war over this issue.

The editor of a major Japanese magazine, meanwhile, approached the White Dragon Society last week with evidence that Hisashi Owada, a judge at the International Court of Justice at the Hague, is a Zionist slave. While in Japan, Owada was responsible for shutting down magazines and blacklisting journalists on behalf of his Zionist slave masters.

Owada is the father of Princess Masako. Masako was living with her foreign ministry boyfriend and rejected out of hand any offers to marry the crown prince. As a result the boyfriend was transferred overseas where he died suddenly in a car accident. Masako then felt obliged to marry the crown prince. The emperor and his family have been blackmailed by the Zionists about this.

Humanity will be set free soon.

4
The White Dragon Society

August 8, 2011. It is Time for Revolution

Anybody who is still self-aware, understands that Western civilization has been hijacked by gangsters: - a bunch of not very intelligent and extremely vicious gangsters. It is time we force them out of power and set humanity free.

Western civilization used to have the moral high ground on such issues as academic freedom, human rights, scientific progress, environmental protection etc. Now it is rightly seen as a civilization hijacked by a criminal class that advocates endless war against manufactured enemies. The crimes of the ruling class of most Western countries are provable in any real court of law. It is time to bring them to justice.

The problem is that the highest levers of power in both the political and judicial systems in the West have been taken over by criminals. When the system can no longer provide justice, then revolution is the only answer. We need to arrest at most a few thousands, probably in fact only a few dozen, oligarchs in order to save Western civilization from the criminal, fascist class that has used murder, bribery and lies to seize power.

As things stand over 90% of humanities savings is being devoted to murder and war. The so-called leaders of the West have no vision for the future but war. They wish to use these wars to enslave humanity and establish themselves as living gods.

The White Dragon Society has a different vision. We propose using humanity's savings to end war, end poverty and stop environmental destruction. After that, humanity can be set on a path of exponential expansion into the universe. Our savings and our future planning can be devoted to such attainable goals as increased longevity, improved human abilities, free energy, the creation of new eco-systems, the expansion of life in all its forms and anything else scientifically possible and morally permissible that we can dream of.

The White Dragon Foundation has been set up in order to attain these goals. It will carry them out by means of a meritocratically staffed international economic planning agency.

The Foundation is now soliciting donations in order to make this possible. All donations can be sent to the following account:

The White Dragon Foundation
Mizuho Bank,
Kichijoji Branch 2-2-13 Kichijoji Honcho, Musashino-City, Japan 180-0004
Swift Code: MHBKJPJT
Branch Number: 246
Account Number 1378636

Please note the bank charges a $50 processing fee for each overseas donation. For that reason, we are not soliciting donations from people of limited means.

5
Global Debt Forgiveness

Universal debt forgiveness and the imminent global debt jubilee.

• When debt is fraudulent, debt forgiveness is the logical and only remedy.

• Debt or credit which cannot be paid back is never an asset; it is always a liability.

• All debt which charges a percentage originates in delusion. Debt grows exponentially indefinitely; income and other financial growth cannot do this.

• The total amount of money in circulation today in the West can only pay for a tiny fraction of the total private and public debt in the West. This fact is evidence of systemic fraud.

• Debt is manufactured through fraudulent means to reward a creative criminal élite.

• If the intention of a financial transaction tied to a loan, or tied to a financial inducement, is extortion, if it is, in effect, an élite bankster scheme to bamboozle the borrower with small print or to blind him with science, that loan or inducement, should be struck off the record immediately and completely. The debt was not incurred with the informed consent of the borrower.

The debt did not benefit the borrower. And the élite lender was well aware of these facts when the loan papers were signed.

• You cannot solve the debt problem by issuing more debt. You solve the debt problem by cancelling, completely, all national, corporate and personal debt. You do this simultaneously across the planet, and you do it permanently.

You don't need a slide rule, a set of log tables or a high frequency trading algorithm to see the light. Everyone on Main Street now knows that the Western cabal's fixation with fiat-paper capitalism is a busted flush. Debt does not work as the basis of a global financial system.

Behind the scenes, all the indications are that universal debt forgiveness is set to be announced. A global debt jubilee is waiting in the wings. The Doctrine of Odious Debts has been spectacularly revisited. The default position of the global financial system is to be permanently reset. The vaults are stocked. The precious metals are audited. The new gold-backed regional currencies are printed, minted and ready.

The most recent catalyst for change has been Iraq. Before the Western cabal's US-UK war of occupation and plunder began in Iraq in March 2003, Iraqi exiles expressed the hope that in a post-Saddam democratic Iraq, there would be a fair and equitable disposition of Saddam's debts.

These Iraqis wanted the future administration of Iraq and the international community to review the debts accumulated under Saddam's régime. Those loans which had been used for benign purposes should be restructured and paid back by Iraq over a prudent time period. Those loans which were used for objectionable purposes and which did nothing to enhance the well-being or prosperity of the Iraqi population at large, should be struck off the record immediately and completely.

This illustrates one of the core principles of debt forgiveness. Why should Iraqis be forced to repay the US, the British, the French, the Germans, the Russians, and all the others who had financially supported Saddam's oppression of them?

The Iraqi argument for debt forgiveness had a sound basis in law. It reflects the century-old legal principle of the Doctrine of Odious Debts.

The Doctrine of Odious Debts was created to further international finance by limiting the ability of governments to repudiate debts. Three conditions had to apply before a sovereign state could repudiate a debt:

(1) The debt must have been incurred without the informed consent of the citizenry of the state.

(2) The debt must not have benefitted the citizenry of the state.

(3) The lender must have been aware of conditions (1) and (2) at the time that the loan papers were signed.

The United States employed these principles after the Spanish-American War to repudiate the Cuban debts.

If a despotic power incurs a debt which is manifestly not for the needs of the State, or not in the plain interest of the State, but is a debt incurred solely to strengthen the position of the despotic cabal as a self-serving faction within that State, the debt is odious. The debt is not an obligation for the nation; it is a cabal debt, a personal debt of the cabal which incurred it. And the debt falls with the fall of the cabal.

The Doctrine of Odious Debts not only promotes accountability, it promotes democracy in the debtor state as, one by one, the nature of the inherited debts are articulated in a public legislature.

The Doctrine of Odious Debts also promotes democracy in creditor states. In Canada and most European nations, the lending of state enterprises is generally hidden from taxpayers. Canada's export credit agency, Export Development Canada, for example, is exempt from Canada's Access to Information law.

In the case of Iraq, state agencies from France, Germany and Russia may have made questionable loans. Under an odious debt process, they would need to establish that they acted with due diligence to be entitled to repayment. Knowing this, they would be less likely to make questionable loans in the future.

Debt forgiveness and the Doctrine of Odious Debts also applies to individuals. The same principles have legal traction on loans or structured financial inducements made by financial institutions such as banks, mortgage lenders, insurance companies, stock-trading entities, energy conglomerates and pharmaceutical firms.

If the intention of the financial transaction tied to

the loan, or tied to the financial inducement, is extortion, if it is, in effect, an élite scheme to bamboozle the borrower with small print or to blind him with science, that loan or inducement, should be struck off the record immediately and completely. The debt was not incurred with the informed consent of the borrower. The debt did not benefit the borrower. And the lender was well aware of these facts when the loan papers were signed.

Universal debt forgiveness is on the way as an essential precursor to the planet's new gold-backed financial system. It has deep historical roots and powerful support in natural law. This imminent global debt jubilee is organically related to the disbursement of The World Global Settlement Funds, to the long-planned public NESARA announcements, and to the opening of Pandora's Suitcase.

When debt is fraudulent, debt forgiveness is both the logical and the only remedy for the situation. Whatever the name you give to the process — erasure, repudiation, abolishment, cancellation, jubilee — debt forgiveness will eventually have to emerge at the forefront of global efforts to solve the ongoing systemic financial crisis.

The only way to erase counterfeit money and counterfeit assets amounting to hundreds of trillions of dollars is to erase the debts associated with these fake assets. They are not toxic assets. They are fake assets.

Debt forgiveness accomplishes two important things. First, it eliminates the increasing and outsized portion of productive enterprise which is being employed to pay off unproductive obligations. Second, it clears the ground for new opportunities, new thinking, creative invention and positive entrepreneurialism.

Stentorian calls for austerity are nothing more than the delusional efforts of a fraudulent bankster status quo to avoid the consequences of its own error and fraud. The élite demands for austerity are a self-serving effort to kick the profit-can down the road in perpetuity. So bedazzled by the false wealth created by debt multiplication and its concomitant fantasy of ever-higher returns, the fraudulent bankster status quo continues to be stupidly amazed that ordinary people in the street are not spending money, and that the national economy is not picking up.

Productive human wealth has been trapped by establishment banksters in a web of parasitic theft, counterfeiting, liability evasion, non-regulation, and prosecutorial non-accountability. All the fundamental attributes of a functioning exchange economy have been warped to reward creative criminals.

Fabricated, or parasitic, so-called "wealth" destroys value by diluting the value of real productive wealth. Debt or credit which cannot be paid back is never an asset; it is always a liability. That some people in the market can be fooled into buying such liabilities and thus generate sale profits and transaction fees is derisible.

The operating models upon which the modern debt nexus is historically based have no organic contact with reality. They assume unlimited growth and an unlimited ability to pay. When matched against the reality of real people paying ten times their salary for mortgages, which actually add more money owed to their principal (with negative amortization), require no money down, and set up balloon payments — large step-ups in payments after a few years — there is no possible way such people could not default within a predictable timespan.

Systemically, all debt which charges a percentage originates in delusion. Debt grows exponentially indefinitely; income and other growth cannot do this. This leads to a widening condition where the fruits of productive growth devoted to interest payments increase until those fruits are entirely consumed. Once this happens, stores of wealth (hard assets) begin to be cannibalised to make up the difference. You can see this now in Middle America where, absurdly, people are having to liquidate their retirement accounts to pay for their current cost of living.

The problem is compounded by a privately owned Federal Reserve syndicate which lends money into circulation at interest, and then allows the multiplication of this consumer debt-money liability through fractional reserve banking.

The total amount of money in circulation today can pay for only a tiny fraction of the total private and public debt. This fact alone is evidence of a kind of systemic fraud. This is why debt forgiveness makes not only moral, but also rational and mathematical sense. Finances require balancing to be coherent. There has to be some way to redress the systemic imbalance in Western macrofinance. There has to be some way to zero the scales in order to get an accurate weight of value, and to re-establish healthy value creation.

The problem with debt is that it creates scarcity. Scarcity stimulates fear. Fear drives manic competition. And manic competition favors opportunism, collusion, and concentrations of power. These élite concentrations of power translate into establishment abuse. The inevitable result is a visible collapse of legitimacy within the economic system. This is what is being seen now, all over the Western World, by Joe Public and his missus.

Debt forgiveness recognises the inherent, systemic, mathematical inability to make good on debts, and (or) the naked fact that the debt itself was manufactured through fraudulent means.

The situation is plain. You cannot solve the debt problem by issuing more debt. You solve the debt problem by cancelling, completely, all national, corporate and personal debt. You do this simultaneously across the planet, and you do it permanently. And then you recapitalise the whole bangshoot using an established resource base such as The World Global Settlement Funds and the associated US Dollar Refunding Project.

This next bit sounds exotic. But in future years it may well sound like a blinding glimpse of the obvious. You don't establish the value of something by sticking it in a market. You establish the value of something by giving it away free and seeing what social value accrues as that something is used locally to energise cooperative livelihoods and free barter.

Interestingly, the core idea of global debt forgiveness is not restricted to the benevolent ivory towers of future economic utopians. It is beginning to be talked about, in public, by national parliamentarians.

At the end of August 2011, in Ireland, the Irish Finance Minister, Michael Noonan, had to respond to organised calls for debt forgiveness in connection with his EuroZone nation's struggling mortgage borrowers. The story was run prominently in the Business section of the Irish Times on Friday 2nd September 2011. Its headline was: "Minister rules out 'free-for-all' debt forgiveness. Noonan insists there is no magic bullet."

NESARA II

6

57-Nation White Dragon Society Alliance Issues Final Warning To Western Cabal Satanists In US, Canada, UK, France and Italy.

Jay Rockefeller, Henry Kissinger, George Bush, Sr., George Bush Jr., and Tony Blair, specifically named as élite proponents of a four billion human genocide plan.

A full transcript of this Benjamin Fulford message can be read here. Benjamin Fulford is a spokesman for the White Dragon Society.

Japan - Tuesday, August 30, 2011

"This is Benjamin Fulford speaking on August 30th 2011. My fellow humans, we have some important news to announce. A meeting took place last week between representatives of fifty seven countries. The meeting took place in a ship in international waters off the coast of Monaco."

"The meeting was forced on to the ship by representatives of the cabal that is now ruling France, Italy, England, Canada and the United States. The representatives of the various governments were presented with unequivocal evidence that the cabal controlling these countries was planning genocide — was planning to murder more than four billion human beings through disease, war and starvation. And a consensus has been made to overthrow these criminals."

"I have a message, now, for Chancellor Merkel of Germany. We would like to ask you, Angela Merkel, to please side with humanity and break away from this murderous cabal. Free the German people from their control. Ask yourself if you face a War Crimes Tribunal in the future, will you have a clear conscience? I believe you will, and I believe that you are on the side of humanity."

"I would also like to ask Prime Minister Cameron of the United Kingdom the same question. Are you sure that you would be able to have a trial at a War Crimes Commission where you would have a clear conscience? I do not think so. I think the murder of citizens of Libya and the stealing of their oil is a crime."

"And President Sarkozy of France, your fellow leaders now know that you entrapped Strauss-Kahn with a maid you sent in cooperation with elements of the Federal Reserve Board, and your dirty tricks are known. And perhaps you should just stay in New Caledonia, I don't think you're going to be welcome in France much longer."

"The government of Italy, too, you have to understand there's not going to be a fascist coup, there's not going to be a fascist world government."

"Remember this, we know who these people are. It's the Trilateral Commission, the Bilderbergers and the Council on Foreign Relations. We're talking about a few hundred old men. We're talking about George Bush Senior and Junior, we're talking about Henry

Kissinger, Senator Jay Rockefeller, we're talking about Tony Blair. We know who these people are. We know that you are planning to kill four billion people. It's not going to happen."

"The Pentagon and the agencies are now on our side. We are going to break into the Global Collateral Accounts and make sure that you cannot cut off the money supplies to the White Hats."

"You must surrender. If you do not surrender, you will lose any chance you have. And that chance is shrinking by the day - of being able to appear before a Truth and Reconciliation Committee in exchange for forgiveness of your crimes. That time is running out. You are going to go to gaol, or worse, if you do not stand aside."

"Humanity is tired of your endless wars. We know that ninety per cent of human savings is going towards murder and crimes against humanity. We don't want this any more. You are not going to be financed. You are being cut off financially from the rest of the world. Your days are numbered."

"We want freedom. We want the ability to use our resources to find ways to improve the environment, to end poverty, to end war, to explore the universe, to make us all happier and healthier. We are tired of your incompetent rule. You must stand aside."

"We have the governments of fifty seven countries behind us now. The Japanese government will be with us soon. And I believe that the sooner you realise that your days are numbered, the better it is for you. This is your final warning. Thank you."

"My fellow humans, you will be free soon. You're

going to be born into an age of wonder. There'll be many, many good things will happen. Once these murderers are out of power, you will find so many wonderful things in your life. I guarantee you this. This is not pie in the sky. This is real. Thank you."

http://tinyurl.com/3qhemkl

7
The Biggest Event!
- In 2000 Years

A David Wilcock Interview with Benjamin Fulford:

80 DIFFERENT COUNTRIES HAVE NOW FORMED AN ALLIANCE AGAINST THE ONE WORLD ORDER/NAZI-ESQUE CABAL

Two huge underground cities were destroyed on August 23rd, 2011 — which may be seen by historians as the critical moment in which the undeclared war was won.

NUCLEAR STRIKES AGAINST UNDERGROUND BASES

Recently, these sources reported that the earthquakes that occurred in Colorado and in the Washington DC area, surrounding August 22nd and 23rd, were, in fact, nuclear strikes against underground military bases. These bases were built by the US government, ostensibly since the early 1960s, at the cost of trillions of dollars of undocumented taxpayer money going into these "black projects."

I was absolutely astonished when it was confirmed that this attack did happen.

THEY NEVER IMAGINED IT COULD HAPPEN

If you haven't understood the gravity or the implications of what I'm telling you right now, it's important to point one thing out.

These guys never imagined that these underground facilities could ever have been attacked. Ever.

So what has happened here is a seismic shift in this insider war — arguably as significant as the nuking of Hiroshima and Nagasaki in World War II.

CODE RED — ON A NEED-TO-KNOW BASIS

There is great significance in this happening. I was astonished at the depth of detail I have been able to get from my own sources about what happened.

I've been told that the situation is now considered Code Red. However, it is also being withheld from most of the people in these [classified] programs. It's on a need-to-know basis.

Even the sources I am in contact with, all except for one, did not have the need-to-know basis high enough to know why this happened. Or who was responsible for it!

MINING FOR INFORMATION

So the only thing we know is that the "powers that were", as I like to call them, have been putting out stories on the Internet about this event.

What they're actually doing is trying to mine for information. They want to find out who knows what.

And I'm astonished that my own sources lack the knowledge that Benjamin Fulford has been putting out as to who is responsible for this… and why it was done.

UP TO SIXTY THOUSAND DEATHS — AND NO INSIDER IS SAFE

My intelligence suggests it is possible that as many as 30,000 people were in each of these two underground cities at the time that the explosions went off.

So we're talking about potentially 60,000 deaths.

We're also talking about the potential that anyone else working for these programs who is in one of these facilities, which could either be underground or possibly off-world, such as in a space station on the Moon or elsewhere… is now totally unguarded and alone.

They are not going to be protected. They are not safe. And their superiors are not informing them of the risk they are now in by being in those locations.

SET THE RECORD STRAIGHT

I want to set the record straight. I want to get the man to talk to you, the public, and hear firsthand what is going on, who did this, why they did this, and what the implications of it are.

So Ben, that's my intro. Let's hear from you now. I'm very interested in this.

BRETTON WOODS SET THE STAGE

BF: There has been a very esoteric battle over control of the dollar printing machine for the global financial system.

At the end of World War II, at the 1944 Bretton Woods accords, Britain, France and the US were given the right to control the world's currency.

They were supposed to have had a Marshall Plan to develop Africa and Asia, and Europe as well.

They reneged on their promise, and instead started to fake a "cold war" with the Soviet Union — which was designed to support the military industries.

77 NON-ALIGNED NATIONS SET UP GLOBAL COLLATERAL ACCOUNTS

The group of 77 non-aligned nations pooled their assets… all their wealth, their gold and other valuables… and set up some global collateral accounts.

They wanted to use this money to start the Marshall Plans for Asia and Africa.

KENNEDY TRIED TO END THE FED — AND THE COLD WAR

President Kennedy agreed to go along with this after he found out that there was a group trying to get the Soviet Union and the United States to annihilate each other. This was the Cuban Missile Crisis.

The historical accord is called the Hilton Green Memorial. This is available to any serious researcher in financial history.

President Sukarno, of Indonesia, was the signatory for the countries. He was going to give Kennedy — they gave Kennedy 140,000 tons of gold.

Kennedy passed a law allowing Congress, not the Federal Reserve Board, to create dollars from these gold-backed global collateral accounts given to the United States.

Kennedy also said, "Let's go to the Moon, to stimulate industry, instead of waging this Cold War. Let's develop the poor countries and let's develop space instead of having this fake Cold War."

KENNEDY WAS ASSASSINATED IN 1963 — AND THE CLOCK RAN OUT

Kennedy did issue a lot of money, but he was assassinated. And, as you know, the public space program disappeared in the 1970s, when that funding ran out. It stopped completely. And President Sukarno was hounded from office.

The international agreement that left Britain, France and the United States in charge of the world's financial system expired in 1994. That is why they wound down the Soviet Union.

After 1994, there was no accord at the very top level of the world's financial system about who would be next in charge. There was a split in the ranks

CHINA AND THE NON-ALIGNED NATIONS WANTED FINANCIAL CONTROL

The Chinese and the non-aligned nations were pressuring the oligarchs who had been running things since World War II to hand over control of the dollar printing press — the financial system — but they were reluctant.

The international court of justice at the Hague was sued by the Chinese over gold that the Federal Reserve Board owners sold to them.

THE FED HAD TO PAY UP ON SEPTEMBER 12, 2001

The Federal Reserve Board owners lost this lawsuit, and they were told to hand over the gold, starting on September 12, 2001.

Instead, on September 11, 2001, as you all know, they started this huge, fake, global war on terror. It was part of an attempt at controlling the planet by the fascist groups of World War II.

THEY WANTED GLOBAL FASCISM — AND 90% FEWER PEOPLE

The Nazis and their fascist sympathizers in the US, and England, and Italy, along with a group within the military, in Congress, and in the Vatican, were going to set up a global fascist government.

At the same time, they believed that there were too many people. Especially too many inferior brown-type people.

They wanted to reduce the world's population by 90 percent.

DW: This is documented?

BF: Yes, it's very well documented.

I was invited to join this group by Heizo Takanaka, who was the Japanese finance minister for five years. I have a tape recording of this to prove it.

THEY INTENDED TO HIDE UNDERGROUND AFTER NUKING THE PLANET

They were planning to hide in these underground bases after they set off a nuclear holocaust.

The original plan was to start a nuclear war between Israel and Iran, and use that as an excuse to set up martial law in the G7 countries.

This new military strength would then be used to prepare for war against China.

RUSSIA AND CHINA CUT THEM OFF

This plan fell apart when Russia kicked them out — and Putin re-asserted independence for Russia.

That removed their control — the oil industry — and made that whole plan not work.

The Chinese also stopped buying US treasuries for a while to put pressure on this group.

THEY OFFERED TO PARTNER WITH CHINA IN WORLD DICTATORSHIP

So they switched strategies. Instead, they tried to cozy up to China and offer them a world dictatorship… in partnership with this group.

That's why in public you saw Obama visit China in 2009 and offer a "G2" Deal. This is how you can confirm this.

THEY ARE BEING CUT OFF — AND ARE RUNNING OUT OF MONEY

In any case, this group that carried out the 9/11 attacks has been under increasing pressure, and isolation, at the very highest levels.

They are running out of money. They are being cut off.

WHAT ABOUT THE "MISSING" 2.3 TRILLION DOLLARS?

DW: Ben, right before September 11, a lot of people forgot about this. Donald Rumsfeld goes on national television and says that they "lost" 2.3 trillion dollars from the Pentagon over the previous decade.

Does that have anything to do with this gold thing you are talking about?

BF: Oh yeah.

FINANCING "MURDER INCORPORATED"

That money was used to finance Blackwater — a private army not controlled by the Pentagon.

The Pentagon would not let themselves be controlled by this cabal. So the cabal was trying to do what the Nazis did in World War II — create an elite SS corps that could bully the regular military.

That was where that money went to, as far as my sources are concerned.

DW: Wow.

BF: In any case, we were contacted by smugglers, drug smugglers…

DW: Could you just say who "We" is, for a minute?

THE WHITE DRAGON SOCIETY — MANY GROUPS COLLABORATING

BF: "We" is a group of us who are involved in the

fight to overthrow this fascist cabal.

It includes members of the CIA, the Pentagon, the intelligence agencies, and various other groups, including Asian secret societies.

We use the name White Dragon. There is another group that calls themselves the White Hats.

We all have the same goal, which is to get this insane group of people out of power.

WHY FULFORD?

DW: Some of the criticism I have seen from people on the Internet is, "If this group is so vast and so powerful to fight this cabal, why is Benjamin Fulford the only one talking about this?"

BF: These people like their secrecy — and I am a spokesperson.

When you go to the White House, there is only one voice they give to the public. They prefer to work behind the scenes.

You've got to realize that we're dealing in a world where they use assassination like most of us use tissue paper.

DW: For sure.

IT IS VERY DANGEROUS TO STAND AGAINST THE CABAL

BF: I've had about six murder attempts, myself. One of my colleagues, a CIA guy, was recently poisoned with ricin by these guys.

Another one of our members, in Switzerland, has guards around his house, and they just shot someone last week near his house who was trying to kill him.

Before that, they found a Mafioso by the name of

Vincenzo Mazzamaro who had a gun and a sophisticated lock-picking device, and was trying to get into his place.

DW: Wow.

BF: We're dealing with some very dangerous people. That's why there is a need for secrecy.

FULFORD IS BILINGUAL AND HIGH PROFILE IN ASIA THANKS TO FORBES

DW: I've also speculated that the following reason why these Asian groups entrusted you with this responsibility.

You are in Japan, and you're a "gaijin" — a foreigner, a white person. You have the background of being a distinguished editor for Forbes Magazine.

You are bilingual, you speak fluent Japanese. There are several videos you have released now that show that.

This might have been part of what gave you this platform to give these Asian secret societies a voice.

Would you say that is correct?

WHY WASN'T JAPAN USING ITS MONEY TO HEAL THE PLANET?

BF: What happened in my case was that I asked a very simple and obvious question when I was at Forbes.

The Japanese people — including both public and the private sector — have about 8 trillion dollars worth of assets overseas.

DW: Eight trillion dollars?

BF: Yeah. That's in the public record. You can go to the finance ministry homepage and the numbers are there.

According to the UN development report, you need 400 billion to stop environmental destruction and 200 billion to end poverty.

So I'm saying, "Hey, you guys, why don't you end poverty and stop environmental destruction?"

DW: Okay, hold on, hold on.

BF: It's a no-brainer!

400 BILLION? THAT'S IT?

DW: 400 billion is all it takes to completely stop environmental destruction? How is that possible?

BF: That's an annual budget. This is the UN development report. You'd have to go through their experts and find out how they did those numbers.

DW: Okay. But that's public domain.

So the eight trillion is vastly more than what it would take to end poverty and stop environmental destruction.

BF: Yeah.

JAPANESE REVENUE DRAINED FROM RECON-STRUCTION DEBTS

[Wilcock note: Elsewhere, Fulford said he found that a significant percentage of Japanese revenue was being paid to the oil cabal — thanks to exploitive reconstruction contracts with high interest rates that were signed after World War II.

These contracts were enforced with bribery, blackmail, death threats and assassinations of Japanese government officials who didn't agree.]

90 PERCENT OF WORLD SAVINGS ABSORBED BY US MILITARY

BF: The other thing is that if you look at the statistics, you realize that 90% of the world's savings is being sucked out of the system by the US military-industrial complex.

DW: How do you prove that?

BF: I was a financial journalist for 25 years. This is all public-record stuff.

DW: Ninety percent of the US budget is going to the military!

BF: There's an easy way to check. Just look at the US external trade deficit and compare it to the US military budget. You'll find an amazing similarity over the years.

DW: (Laughs)

BF: That's for the simple reason that the military does not produce tradable goods. They are a parasitic entity on the world economy.

WHY NOT HEAL THE WORLD AND COLONIZE SPACE?

What I said was simply, "Look. Why don't you just stop paying for this military?" I told this to the Asians – "and instead ask them to end poverty and environmental destruction and set them to exploring space?"

It's the sort of thing that's just common sense.

DW: Okay, Ben, your audio just cut out on that last sentence. Missing content was replaced in brackets.

BF: I think that is common sense.

DW: Okay.

ASSASSINATION ORDERS

BF: An assassination order came out for me. The South Korean secret police informed the Chinese that there was an order to have me killed.

You can check. My colleague Paul Klebnikov, the Moscow bureau chief for Forbes Magazine, was shot nine times outside of his apartment in Moscow.

He was still alive when the ambulance came an hour later. He got to the hospital and he was put in the hospital elevator. The elevator was stopped for eight minutes — and he died in the elevator.

He was investigating a member of this same group that I was.

He was investigating Boris Berezovsky, one of the oil tycoons.

I was investigating Heizo Takenaka — but they all go back to the same cabal.

DW: Right.

THE WAR ON TERROR WAS OBVIOUSLY A FAKE

BF: In any case, the South Koreans told the Chinese that an assassination order was out for me. This was because of my publicly calling for the Asians to stop spending their savings on this vast military machine.

You have got to remember, during the Cold War they actually had this anti-Communism excuse.

But, the War on Terror was so obviously fake that it was just ridiculous to anybody who does any serious research or investigation.

DW: Right.

CHINESE SECRET SOCIETY OFFERS PROTECTION

BF: I got invited to join a Chinese secret society that offered me protection from this assassination order — and that's how I found myself in this secret world of financial power.

The group that offered me protection was the group

that was behind the non-aligned nations.

It crosses borders. If you think in terms of countries, you don't understand how these people work.

They have big factions in China, in the US, and in Europe — both against and for them. It crosses borders.

If you think in terms of nation-states, you won't understand how these groups work.

CHINESE FIGHT FINANCIAL BATTLE BY BUYING REAL ASSETS

In any case, a financial battle started. There were many, many public salvos.

In 2006, the Chinese wanted to use their dollars to do something other than buy Treasuries.

They tried to buy the oil company Unocal. Congress passed a law saying they could not.

So then they took their dollars and they went to Africa, South America, and everywhere, and started spending them on real things — like mines and agricultural land and commodities.

Not virtual things — like fancy and impossible to understand derivatives products, which are basically con jobs.

DW: Ponzi schemes. Yeah.

BF: Yeah.

FOOD AND OIL PRICES INCREASED BY CABAL

The other group tried to retaliate by jacking up food and oil prices.

Remember there were hunger riots in 33 countries at one point.

DW: Yeah.

BF: An economist at the World Bank pointed out

that the reason people were going hungry was that they were paying farmers to grow oil [ethanol made from corn] instead of food.

That put an end to that.

2008 LEHMAN SHOCK WAS ASIAN COUNTER-ATTACK

Then there was a counter-attack.

The [leaders of the cabal] were told that we would no longer accept dollars printed within the United States.

That's what you know of as the Lehman crisis.

76 PERCENT DROP IN JAPANESE CAR EXPORTS TO THE US

You can check this in the public record.

If you look at Japanese export statistics, from October or November 2008, after the Lehman shock, you will see something like a 76% year-to-year drop in Japanese car exports to the US.

This was the Japanese and other people saying, "You can no longer use paper to buy stuff from the rest of the world. You have to trade with real things."

Of course, your public was not let in on this.

DW: That's where I think people's brain is going to get busted. Nobody publicly knows that this Lehman shock had anything to do with Asia.

BF: Yeah, I know. The way you can check it is to look at the export-import statistics after the Lehman shock.

The other way to check it is to look at the Baltic Dry Index. That's the price of shipping.

90 PERCENT DROP IN THE PRICE OF SHIPPING

You will see that the price of shipping dropped 90%

right after the Lehman shock.

DW: Wow.

BF: That's because the ships were no longer going to the US, full of stuff, and then leaving empty [with nothing but worthless paper and IOUs].

These are ways people can verify what I'm saying with public-record information.

DW: Good. Okay.

NORWAY SHOOTING WAS AN ATTEMPT TO EXTORT 1.5 TRILLION

BF: Getting back to the blowing up of the underground bases, this group was being cut off more and more at a high level, and they were running out of money.

They were trying to extort money from various countries.

They killed the youth group of the ruling party in Norway — that was the Norway attacks — because they were trying to extort the 1.5 trillion-dollar oil fund the Norwegian government controls.

They were saying, "Hey, we're going to kill you if you don't hand over your money."

DW: They were desperately trying to find cash.

BF: Yeah. They invaded Libya to take over their oil fields, because the Libyans told them, "We're not going to give you oil for your paper anymore."

DW: Hmmm.

NUCLEAR BOMB SMUGGLED INTO JAPAN WITH 70 KILOS OF MARIJUANA

BF: In the case of Japan, again, I have sources who are actually drug smugglers. They have been selling drugs in Japan for 70 years.

These are CIA types. The CIA drug-smuggling division.

They told me that a nuclear bomb had been brought in with their latest shipment of drugs.

This was a 70-kilo shipment of adulterated Thai marijuana that was brought in through Okinawa.

They found a nuclear bomb mixed in with it.

And of course, with these guys, smuggling drugs is one thing, but smuggling nuclear weapons is another.

They told the police, and they told me. I made it public.

They followed the bomb as far as the North Korean citizens' association headquarters in Tokyo.

FOUR NUKES STOLEN FROM THE RUSSIAN SUB 'KURSK'

I have independent confirmation from a Mr. Paul Lane, of Pentagon military intelligence — he was a part of the 'Men Who Stare At Goats' group —that four nuclear weapons were stolen from the Russian submarine Kursk after it sank.

I think it was in 2000 or something.

It was one of those nuclear weapons that was smuggled in [to Japan].

DW: Stolen by who, though?

BF: This is the Odessa group. The Nazi group. The one that was trying to set up a fascist world government — a Fourth Reich.

DW: Okay. How did they get to the Kursk to get these nukes out?

BF: I don't know the technical details, but they have submarine bases in various parts of the world. I assume it was from one of these submarine bases.

WHY STEAL NUKES IF YOU CAN BUILD YOUR OWN?

DW: The next question, then, would be why would they need to get it from the Kursk if they are powerful enough to make their own?

BF: The public nuclear devices are under strict safety protocols. You can't just take them and then blow them up somewhere. There are too many people involved in the chain of command.

They tried to do that.

MINOT AIR FORCE BASE INCIDENT: FAILED SMUGGLING ATTEMPT

There were incidents where [the good guys] just barely stopped a nuclear…

DW: Right. Like the Minot Air Force Base incident.

BF: Yeah, exactly.

DW: The soldiers did a mutiny and would not commit this "Broken Arrow". That's what they called it in code terms.

[Insiders attempted to smuggle out a nuclear weapon from Minot AFB. Several of these heroes died as a result of standing up against this plan and refusing to allow the nuclear weapon to be stolen.]

BF: There you go. What they needed was some nuclear weapons that were not under any official gov't control.

DW: Okay.

JAPANESE SHIP DRILLING TEN KILOMETERS AT EXACT EPICENTER

BF: There was a Japanese drilling ship known as the Chikuyu Maru that can drill ten kilometers into the seabed.

They were drilling at the exact epicenter of the earthquake.

We had an article from January 17 in a local paper saying they were drilling there.

They put the bomb in the seabed!

HAND OVER THE CASH — OR TOKYO WILL BE NEXT

This was an attempt to extort money, through terror, from the Japanese.

DW: So they warned Japan that they put the nuke in [the seabed] before they asked for money?

BF: No, they asked for money afterwards.

DW: Oh, wow.

BF: "If you don't do it, next it's Mount Fuji."

DW: For people who don't know, Fujiyama is right around Tokyo, which is the largest population center of Japan.

BF: Yes. That's right.

DW: So basically they are saying they would nuke Tokyo, which is how many million people? Thirty or forty million?

BF: Thirty million or so.

DW: Right. Okay.

JAPANESE PRIME MINISTER HANDED OVER 20 BILLION

BF: The Japanese prime minister [Naoto] Kan originally was so cowardly, he just said, "Oh yeah, all right, we'll sign over money."

He handed over something like two trillion yen, which is about 20 billion dollars. And they gave him a big bribe.

MAJOR BATTLE WAS TRIGGERED IN JAPAN TO REMOVE THE CABAL

The evidence that this was not a natural disaster began piling up.

The result has been a battle here in Japan to remove these people from control.

WHY DO YOU THINK THIS WAS NOT A NATURAL EARTHQUAKE?

DW: Some people might not realize there is any evidence that Fukushima was not a natural disaster. Could you just briefly touch on a couple of points that you think are the most significant?

[Right before the disaster, I published dream data warning of a huge catastrophe that was about to happen. It was stunningly detailed and accurate.]

BF: If you look at the seismic chart, you will see a sudden explosion.

It's not like a natural earthquake, where you have pre-shocks. It was just suddenly huge, and then it started fading down.

COLORADO AND VIRGINIA EARTHQUAKE LINKS

Disclose TV had a collection of links about the Colorado earthquake and its unusual nature:

http://tinyurl.com/3h6ulfn

There was also a quake in Colorado that has some strange anomalies associated with it. This being that even though this quake was reported in the Denver Post, NY Times, Huff Post, and other local papers, it has been de-listed from the USGS.gov site.

http://tinyurl.com/3dobyxf

http://tinyurl.com/3fdqaq6

Here are six strange anomalies associated with the Virginia quake:

1. Unusual, seismically inactive location.
2. Extremely shallow depth — later altered by USGS to a more typical value.
3. Odd seismograph reading. (Air Force insider leaks that it was an underground nuclear explosion.)
4. Shocks felt well over 500 miles from epicenter.
5. "Remarkably low" number of aftershocks.
6. Hurricane Irene was instantly knocked off course.

PLUTONIUM PUT IN FUKUSHIMA A MONTH BEFORE THE ATTACK

BF: There is plenty of evidence [that Fukushima was not a natural earthquake].

The governor of Fukushima province told me they overruled him and put plutonium in reactor number 3.

[This was only] one month before the tsunami incident.

DW: Only a month before?

BF: Yeah.

[The plutonium caused most of the radiation poisoning from the disaster.]

HOUSING COMPANY'S STOCK SHOT UP A MONTH BEFORE THE ATTACK

And then we had a company called Higashi Nippon House. They make cheap housing in northeastern Japan.

Their stock was shooting up in the month before the attack.

You've got to remember: Japan has an aging and shrinking population.

It doesn't make sense for a cheap housing company's stock price to go shooting up like that — unless there was something in the works.

POSSIBLE NUCLEAR ATTACK THREATENED TWO DAYS BEFORE

The other thing is that a group of us recorded a conversation between Kirk Campbell, who is your deputy foreign minister for Asia, and Japanese power broker Ichiro Ozawa — on March 9, 2011.

In this conversation, Campbell asked Ozawa not to split the ruling party and force the formation of a new government. [This could easily have resulted in a loss of cabal control over Japan.]

They said [if he agreed to keep the ruling party intact,] they would give him the rights to zeolite [they owned] in Fukushima province. Zeolite is used to clean up radioactive waste.

This conversation was recorded on March 9 — two days before the tsunami attack.

NETANYAHU PERSONALLY THREATENED NEW NUCLEAR DISASTERS

The other point [came in from] a man by the name of Takemasa Kawase, a Japanese military intelligence officer.

[He] subsequently told me that Israeli prime minister Benjamin Netanyahu phoned Japanese prime minister Naoto Kan after the attack.

[Netanyahu] said that they would cause other nuclear disasters around Japan if they did not start handing over the money.

The chief Mossad agent in Japan, by the way, is a man named Michael Green. He's a nasty piece of work, and we're going to remove him from this country soon.

DW: One question, though.

BF: Yeah, but I want to…

DW: OK, go ahead.

ISRAELI COMPANY WAS IN CHARGE OF SECURITY AT FUKUSHIMA

BF: In order to confirm what this guy told me, I went to check — and an Israeli company was in charge of security at the Japanese nuclear plant.

DW: Oh my gosh!

BF: So I was able to independently confirm that through other sources. This is publicly available information — who was in charge of security at Fukushima. It was an Israeli company.

Now go on. What was your question?

IS ISRAEL A MEMBER OF THE CABAL?

DW: First, then, do you believe that Israel is tied in with this cabal you keep mentioning, in some way?

BF: Not Israel, but a clique at the top of the Israeli government, yes.

Most Israelis I consider to be chumps or victims of these people.

THE CABAL INTENDED TO SACRIFICE THE ISRAELI PEOPLE

For example the cousin of the Shah of Iran, among others, came to us with information that George Bush and his group had given twelve neutron bombs to the government of Iran.

[These were] missiles with neutron bombs on them.

[Elsewhere, Fulford has said these missiles were intended to be used against Israel.

The cabal hoped it would trigger World War III, which would assist them in depopulating the planet and securing greater military control over the people.]

Remember — neutron bombs kill people but leave buildings [and other property] intact.

DW: Well, that's not only treasonous, it sounds crazy.

BF: It is!

IRANIANS TRIED TO GET RID OF THEM – BUT THEY WERE REFUSED

The Iranians said "We don't want them." They put them at the Iraqi border and asked President Obama to please take them off their hands.

Obama refused to listen.

DW: Wow.

[Elsewhere, Fulford has said that the "Pentagon White Hats" intend to restore constitutional government to the US after overthrowing the cabal, and want to keep the elected president in power as this happens.

I support this decision, and feel it is the best move to make in order to keep the public calm as this event finally comes to pass.

I would be cautious in blaming Obama personally for this alleged decision not to remove nukes from Iran without gaining additional information first.

The president is the intended fall-guy to draw attention away from the cabal conspirators behind the scenes. His true power is limited. Even if he did want to retrieve the weapons, he may not have had any choice.

It may also have been seen as a trap — far too

dangerous to risk the lives of top personnel on what could easily have been a suicide mission.]

MOST ISRAELIS WOULD BE HORRIFIED IF THEY KNEW THE TRUTH

BF: Okay? And again, people at the higher level know this is true. In other words, they were going to offer the people of Israel as a kind of ritual sacrifice.

So the Israelis were victims. A lot of them were fooled with Jewish superiority talk, which is really the same as Aryan superiority talk — only you substitute Jew for Aryan.

They were chumps.

Most of the Israelis don't know what is going on, and they would be appalled to hear it. It's about a cabal that is above all that.

DW: And it has no religious affiliation.

THEY ARE ASSOCIATED WITH JUDAISM / CHRISTIANITY / ISLAM

BF: Well, they are associated with the Abrahamistic religions. Let's put it that way.

DW: Going back to Babylon, Mesopotamia, all the way back there?

BF: Well, at least going back to the time of the Caesars.

RELIGION AND FASCISM

Let's remember the word "religion." The etymology of the word "religion" is *religare* in Latin, which means to *re-bind.*

What do you re-bind it into? A fascio. What is a fascio? It is a bundle of sticks, but it is also fascism.

MONOTHEISTIC RELIGION COULD BE USED FOR MASS MIND CONTROL

At its worst, monotheism — as practiced in the Middle Ages, for example — involved singular control over everybody's thoughts.

Remember — in the Middle Ages, if you didn't believe in the official Catholic doctrine, then you and your entire family would be killed — or tortured until you confessed.

DW: Right. That was the Inquisition.

BF: Well, yeah!

THEY'RE MORE SOPHISTICATED NOW — BUT STILL LOSING THE BATTLE

It's much more sophisticated now.

Five companies control all the major English-[speaking] media — including the TV, the newspapers, the radios, the Hollywood studios.

They're trying to get everybody to think the same way — and they're losing [the battle].

9/11, the story there, was just so full of holes and contradictions that they were losing a significant part of their brainwashed audience — including myself, because I was a high-level brainwashee.

DW: Right.

PENTAGON BLEW UP UNDERGROUND BASES TO FIGHT GENOCIDE

BF: In any case, what happened was that there was a group within the Pentagon and the agencies and stuff that realized this plan was insane.

They knew that the plan to kill 90% of humanity was wrong.

They then blew up the underground bases the elites were going to use to hide in when they carried out their nuclear holocaust.

DW: Okay. I want to get back to that, because that is a really central point.

There is one question I want to ask you before we get to that, because that's the conclusion of the discussion.

WHY DOES THE CABAL NEED TO STEAL MONEY?

Why did these guys need money? If they have so much infrastructure, so many assets, and massive political power, why can't they just nakedly exercise power… move men around, move munitions around?

Why do they need money? Why are they going around like a crackhead looking for a fix?

Why are they going to all these different countries and trying to scam money off of them? Why can't they just print dollars and make more money?

BF: Because people aren't accepting their dollars anymore worldwide.

You've got to remember there are 800 US military bases around the world.

If they can't make the payroll for these guys, they're going to be marching out of their bases with food bowls in their hands, begging for food.

DW: Right.

THE ASIANS CUT OFF THE MONEY SUPPLY TO WALL STREET

BF: They're being cut off from their oil, from their other resources. That was their Achilles heel — the control of money.

Their private army was self-financing. They had their own industries and their own income.

The US army is dependent on Wall Street financing. That's why they were dependent on ultimately the Chinese and the Asians, who were financing Wall Street.

YOU CAN BE THE GOOD GUYS AGAIN

That's why I told the Pentagon guys, "You can have a Starship Enterprise future, exploring the Universe and all that kind of stuff. Just work with us.

"We're not going to cut you off. You're not going to end up like the Soviet Union, where you have a general who is now suddenly being forced to drive a taxi in London.

"You can be the good guys again."

A lot of them said, "Hey, I think that's a good idea. We want to be heroes again. We don't want to be the bad guys."

SUPPRESSED TECHNOLOGY INCLUDING 'ANTIGRAVITY' AND 'STARGATES'

DW: You're saying that they have suppressed technology that could bring us into the Starship Enterprise reality.

A third group based in the US military-intelligence establishment proposes a 5-year swords-to-plowshares transformation of the Pentagon.

This group has the potential to develop the over 6,000 patents that have hitherto been suppressed for "national security" reasons.

One technology they possess is anti-gravity. This would make automobiles obsolete and allow roadways to be transformed into gardens.

They claim to control technology that allows the creation of portals into other dimensions.

They claim (we have not seen proof but have heard

this from many credible eye-witnesses) that many so-called underground bases around the world are actually such portals.

Hopefully we will soon be able to see if this is true. If so, the implications are more than mind-boggling.]

5,135 INVENTIONS HAVE BEEN CLASSIFIED

BF: I don't know about [the Starship Enterprise being a reality].

But, we can confirm, according to the American Academy of Sciences, that more than six thousand patents have been suppressed for so-called "security" or "public safety" reasons.

[DW: This data point is in my new book *The Source Field Investigations.* The Federation of American Scientists revealed that 5,135 inventions had been classified by the end of Fiscal Year 2010.

Among other shocking revelations, we now know that any power system that is more than 70-80% efficient at converting energy will automatically be declared 'classified'.]

Some of these [patents] probably need to be suppressed. We don't want everyone to have a backyard nuke, for example.

DW: Sure.

BF: But a lot of them, I'm hearing, were only kept classified because these people were acting like dogs in the manger. They only wanted the elite to have them.

MANY UFOS ARE FAKE

So my understanding is that, for example, a lot of the so-called UFOs are just sophisticated earth-based secret aircraft that aren't available to the public at large.

DW: I would agree with that. Yeah.

ALIEN ABDUCTIONS MAY BE FROM "PLFs" OWNED BY THE CABAL

[In *Hidden Truth, Forbidden Knowledge,* Dr. Steven Greer of the Disclosure Project reveals compelling insider testimony that UFO abductions are being carried out by so-called Programmable Life Forms (PLFs) owned by the cabal.

There are no reports of "alien abduction" prior to the early 1960s with the infamous Betty and Barney Hill case. This appears to be when the PLF technology was first perfected and put into use.

ALL ET CONTACTS IN THE 1950s WERE WITH POSITIVE HUMANS

[Throughout the 1950s, there were extensive reports of people having direct contact with benevolent human-looking ETs who told them of a coming Golden Age.

These ETs appear to be the same people who appeared in ancient civilizations around the world and were labeled as "gods" or "angels."

Many of these 1950s contacts occurred in the US and Canada, and were studied and compiled by Wilbert B. Smith — a Canadian government worker with classified clearance.

An entirely separate set of positive contacts occurred in Italy, and were the subject of the TV documentary "The Friendship Case", in which key firsthand witnesses broke their silence and spoke about the events they experienced.

A great deal of valuable information about both the

US/Canada and Italian contacts can be found in "1950s Human ETs Prepare Us for Golden Age."
http://tinyurl.com/ykbm4b3

BIOLOGICAL ROBOTS USED TO FIGHT THE POSITIVE ETs WITH FEAR

[The development and implementation of PLF technology appears to have been a direct counter-strike by the cabal against the positive contacts of the 1950s.

Greer's contacts confirmed the PLF technology was acquired from ETs — and involves advanced cloning principles to create a "biological robot".

Apparently, a human fetus is grown in an artificial environment, and without the pressure of the womb, it retains fetal proportions and features — including the large eyes, big head and thin body — on into adulthood.

POSITIVE ETs WOULD NOT INTERFERE UNTIL 2012

[According to the Project Camelot testimony of "Mr. X", an employee for a major defense contractor, the positive ETs gave a very important message to the cabal in the early 1950s.

Several top-secret documents revealed that unless the ETs were specifically invited to show up by a majority of the people, and/or their leaders, they could not appear publicly and openly, on any mass scale, until the end of the year 2012.

This was due to their cooperation with a natural cycle in the Earth — which is apparently governed by a meta-intelligence that exists at the planetary, solar, galactic and universal level — namely the Source Field.

The prophecies and workings of this cycle, and its effects on human evolution, are explored in unprecedented new scientific depth in my book *The Source Field Investigations* (SFI).

SFI debuted at #18 on the New York Times bestseller list, increased to #16 the second week and is at #18 for the third week.

Our publisher, Penguin, incidentally, is not part of the cabal, nor the top five media companies. Extensive secrecy was kept around the book until its release to insure it would not be interfered with.

PLFs USED TO TERRIFY PUBLIC AND PREPARE FOR "ALIEN 9/11"

[Apparently the cabal's intention behind the "alien abduction" phenomenon was to terrify the public — and help set the stage for a fake "Alien 9/11".

This fake alien attack has been extensively telegraphed in a multiplicity of different movies — 18 different movies in the recent past alone.

The major media conglomerates are owned by the cabal and produce these "alien invasion" films for propaganda purposes.

ETs ARE NOW COOPERATING WITH EFFORTS TO DEFEAT THE CABAL

[I have sources with additional information that Fulford has only heard about in minor detail.

Namely, ETs have apparently been cooperating with this international resistance group to defeat the cabal.

Fulford leaked this in a prior interview I did with him in November 2010 — which I finally posted here, as an MP3 file, in May 2011.

http://tinyurl.com/63bevwq

These attacks were totally unexpected, as the cabal was led to believe that the ETs had to follow spiritual laws that forbade them from ever intervening — under any circumstances. However, ETs have routinely powered down nuclear missiles and facilities.

Advanced ET technologies are now being used to strike and disable cabal assets. Many examples have been given in my "China's October Surprise" article series.

The joint campaign began last October — and many obvious, public targets were hit, all with zero casualties.

This included the powering-down of 50 Minuteman ICBMs — and top military witnesses have now publicly reported that a cigar-shaped craft was hovering overhead the entire time.

http://tinyurl.com/42sqkvc

This riveting new detail emerged on June 20, 2011, and completely validated what I had said in the China's October Surprise article series since November 2010.

THE UNDERGROUND BASES WERE A MUCH MORE SIGNIFICANT STRIKE

[However, the destruction of these two major underground facilities is far more massive than other attacks that occurred in November and December 2010, and thereafter.

These earlier attacks did apparently wipe out a great deal of individual craft and munitions that the cabal could have used to fake an alien invasion, according to the insiders I have spoken to.

However, it was always done a little here, a little

there — never all at once. This gave the cabal a false hope that they still had a chance, even as their infrastructure crumbled.

It is very likely that the ETs would not have destroyed two entire underground cities on their own. This attack was much, much bigger than anything else had been.

I believe Fulford is correct in saying that the "good guys" in the Pentagon did this themselves — to stop the genocide from taking place.

ONCE WE DEFEAT THE CABAL, WE STOP THE ABDUCTIONS

[Since the cabal is responsible for manufacturing and implementing the PLFs, the "alien threat" appears to be largely generated from within this group.

Therefore, once we defeat the cabal, we stop the abductions… and the UFO cover-up.]

LET'S USE WHAT WE HAVE – TO TRANSFORM THE PLANET

BF: And so, the point is, let's develop these patents in a safe way, and you can have a boom time such as we haven't had in a very long time.

DW: Right. Instead of creating these financial products that are just voodoo, why not actually build infrastructure?

The existing military-industrial complex, I would argue, is probably the only entity on Earth that has the tools, the factories, the infrastructure and the staff to be able to accomplish this.

BF: Yeah! Exactly. And that's why the generals are now on our side.

The people who are not on our side are mostly

bribed politicians in Washington DC, and the Wall Street crowd. So they are being increasingly isolated.

WHY IN THE WORLD DO THEY WANT TO KILL SO MANY PEOPLE?

DW: Now what possible reason could they have — these adversaries? Why in the world do they want to reduce population?

The average person's mind shuts down because they can't conceptualize that anyone would be that evil. So what's their rationale, as far as you see it?

MASS DEATH IS "GOOD FOR THE ENVIRON-MENT"

BF: The story they tell me is, "Look. We're destroying the environment. There's too many people for the planet to support."

CULTIVATING THE HUMAN RACE LIKE GAR-DENERS

The other thing is these people are elitists. They believe in eugenics.

They say too many stupid people are breeding too much.

Useless eaters. All they do is they destroy the environment, and they don't produce anything. They just sit around and watch TV.

We don't need these people. We want to eliminate the weak and the useless, and just keep the elite.

We want to increase and improve the genetic quality of the human race by purging the garbage from the system.

And, we get to save the environment and create a whole new natural ecosystem.

THE GEORGIA GUIDESTONES

The Georgia Guidestones has their philosophy written out. 500 million people on Earth, in harmony with their environment. This is their goal.

THE NAZIS WERE ENVIRONMENTALISTS

People forget that the Nazis were great green people when it came to preserving nature and natural parks, all that kind of stuff. They were really gung ho about it.

In *Mein Kampf,* Hitler wrote that he wanted to enslave the non-white peoples and then kill them. It's right there.

It's the same group. They're the same Nazis. The same philosophy.

[DW: Fulford didn't mention that after World War II, top German scientists were brought over to the US via Project Paperclip.

The rationale was that if the US didn't get them, they would fall into the hands of the Soviet Union, which was far worse.

It is a well-established, documented fact that Prescott Bush was one of Hitler's main bankers and financial liaisons.

A "Business Plot" was attempted in the 1930s, by Prescott Bush and others, that would have led to the overthrow of American constitutional government and the installing of a fascist system patterned off of Hitler and Mussolini.]

THEY WANTED A SMALL, ENSLAVED POPULATION TO PAMPER THEM

The other thing the super-elite were saying was, "Hey, we're really special. We're really smart. We are the elite, and we should rule the planet like God-kings.

We will need about 500 million slaves or so to keep us pampered, but the rest we don't need."

And it's also about control. They don't have the brainwashed control over large parts of the planet.

They realized they weren't going to be able to control these people. So they thought "let's kill them," rather than lose control of the planet.

THE CABAL WANTS YOU TO FEEL HOPELESS — AND DOOMED

DW: Now a lot of people who read about this stuff online, the vast majority in fact — including most of the guests Jeff Rense or Alex Jones would have on — feel there is an incredible sense of futility.

Everyone seems to go with the knee-jerk reaction that all the governments in the world, all the countries in the world, everybody is in on it.

BF: That's where they are being used and turned into controlled opposition. They are trying to numb people to the message.

"Yeah, it's happening, but there is nothing you can do about it. It's inevitable."

That simply is not the case.

DW: Could you explain why that is not the case?

THEY ONLY CONTROL THE G5 COUNTRIES — AND A FEW SHILLS

BF: They only now control the G5 countries.

DW: Which countries are those?

BF: Those countries are Italy, France, England, Germany and the United States.

DW: That's it? You're saying *ALL* the other countries in the world they don't control anymore?

BF: If you look at the countries that accepted the new… I think maybe they've got a few subject countries like Honduras, Columbia and places like that.

MOST OF THE REST OF THE WORLD IS PART OF THE ALLIANCE

If you look at the African Union, they put out their own currency backed by Ghadafy's gold — and they don't support this group.

Or most of the countries in Asia. Russia. China.

DW: What about European countries like Czechoslovakia, Bulgaria, Romania?

BF: They were at this meeting. There was a meeting in Monaco at the end of August.

57 COUNTRIES GATHERED TO DISCUSS HOW TO DEFEAT THE CABAL

57 countries were invited by the Swiss to discuss cutting those people off financially — and creating an international financial boycott against the controllers of the G5.

DW: Now that's an incredible statement you're making. You're saying 57 different countries, including some of these Eastern European countries…

BF: There were representatives from the Netherlands and Canada there too, OK?

DW: Wow. What about South America?

BF: Yeah, of course. And since then, more than 80 countries have signed on.

IT'S GOING TO BECOME PUBLIC

We're reaching a point where it's going to become public. It's going to be on the airwaves. It's going to be on the news. They can't hide it much longer.

DW: Why the hell haven't they made this public

already?

If people are dying, and these guys are trying to fake an alien invasion — that's one thing we keep hearing, that they are trying to do an Alien 9/11 — why haven't they gone public already?

BF: You don't think they've tried?

VERY DIFFICULT TO GET THE TRUTH PUBLISHED IN THE MAINSTREAM

Look, I had a book proposal at the Berlin book fair. Eleven publishing companies wanted that book out there, including five major ones.

They all came back and said they were told by their bosses they couldn't do it.

DW: Wow. [In my case, the president of Dutton Books, a Penguin division, contacted me directly. Hardly anyone saw the *Source Field* book, or its contents, until it was actually published.]

BF: They've had people going and telling everybody I've ever associated with professionally that I had become an insane drug user.

They control the media. You've got to remember that. There are five companies. Five corporations — controlled by people like Rupert Murdoch, Redstone and stuff.

They have a grip over all the TV studios, all the newspapers, the radio stations, Hollywood studios, etc.

THIS IS NOT A GLOBAL ECONOMIC COLLAPSE

DW: So if their economies are going to go down, they can then say it's a global economic collapse.

BF: And it's NOT a global economic collapse!

SEVEN PERCENT WORLD ECONOMIC GROWTH OUTSIDE THE G5

Again, if you look at the public statistics, you will see that if you exclude the G5 countries, the average growth in the world economy last year was seven percent!

DW: Holy crap!

BF: People are booming! It's not a global crisis — it's a crisis among the countries controlled by this cabal.

DW: And it's only the G5 nations! Wow!

BF: Yes! Look at the statistics. It's all there. It's all in the public record.

You just have to look at government websites and check this out.

EVERYTHING IS AVAILABLE IN THE PUBLIC RECORD

There's nothing I'm saying — including the plan to kill 90 percent of the world's population — that is not in the public record. It's in their own writings!

We have countless confessions. Wernher Von Braun, the guy behind the Apollo projects, said on his deathbed that they were going to use a fake alien invasion as an excuse for genocide.

It's crazy stuff, I know — but it's provable!

These people don't think like normal humans. I guess it was Herbert Hoover — no, J. Edgar Hoover — who said, when a conspiracy is so BIG, people's minds boggle and they go into denial.

In any case, these cabal people are coming down. We've got…

DW: (crosstalk) Right. Now you said something that

is very provocative.

TELL US MORE ABOUT THIS INTERNATIONAL MEETING

You said that there is this meeting that happened, with I believe you said 57 different countries, was it?

BF: Yes.

DW: And this happened in Monaco?

BF: Yes. And it was taken on board a ship which went into international waters. According to two witnesses, senator Jay Rockefeller showed up and tried to break into the meeting — and he was physically ejected.

THE CABAL SENT IN BLACK HELICOPTERS AND WERE CHASED OUT

Two black helicopters appeared above the ship during the meeting, and they were chased away by harrier jets.

DW: Now these black helicopters were like Apaches with weapons on them?

BF: I don't know the details. I just heard that there were two helicopters, and there was a danger that they were going to use some kind of electro-magnetic weapon against the ship.

DW: Oh, like scalar technology kind of stuff. Yeah.

BF: And I know that they were chased away by two harrier jets.

DW: Wow!

BF: US military jets.

THEY WOULD HAVE KILLED EVERYONE — AND TRIED TO MAINTAIN CONTROL

DW: If they had succeeded with those helicopters, what do you think might have happened there? Would everybody have just died?

BF: Well, they would have killed all the representatives. Then they would have said, "Hey, we're in charge, and if you try to go against us, we'll kill you."

This is what they've been doing ever since World War II.

HOW COULD THEY COVER UP A MASS KILLING OF THIS SCOPE?

DW: If so many persons of interest died at once, wouldn't that become a massive international incident that would require investigation anyway?

BF: They have done this before. The Titanic was sunk deliberately to get rid of six hundred senior financiers who were opposed to the taking over of the Federal Reserve Board.

DW: Wow!

BF: They would come up with some story about the 'Tragedy of Monaco'. And the kool-aid drinkers out there would believe it!

I'm sorry, but that's how it is.

[DW: Undoubtedly, the helicopters would have planted and detonated explosives on the boat after neutralizing everyone, and then blamed it on terrorists — and used the incident in an attempt to further their political goals.]

THREE DIFFERENT SOURCES CONFIRMED THE MEETING

DW: Were you at this meeting yourself, Ben?

BF: No. A close colleague of mine was there. And, I confirmed it from two other people who were there, who aren't related to that colleague of mine.

DID ANY OLD WORLD ORDER MEMBERS GET TO ATTEND THE MEETING?

DW: Now what about people from the Trilateral Commission, Bilderberg, or Council on Foreign Relations?

BF: They were deliberately excluded.

DW: Any one of them, no matter who?

BF: No matter who! If they were a member, they weren't allowed.

DW: And that's also why Jay Rockefeller wasn't allowed in.

BF: That's right.

BILDER-BUST

Remember the Bilderberger meeting that took place in June, in St. Moritz, Switzerland this year?

It was supposed to last until Tuesday. They had to all flee on Sunday night, because they were about to be arrested by the Swiss.

DW: Whoa! I never heard that before.

BF: Well, it's there!

SWISS PARLIAMENT MEMBER BEATEN — AND CALLS IN THE COPS

A Swiss lawmaker tried to get into the site and he was beaten up.

He went to the Swiss government and said "I'm a Swiss member of parliament, in my own country, and they beat me up and threw me out. That's illegal."

They said "Yes. We'll go arrest them." They all had to pack their suitcases and flee on Sunday night — before being arrested on Monday.

DW: So this would have been like a paramilitary swat team that would have swept in.

BF: Well yeah — the police authority.

DW: Right.

BF: So there you go. The Bilderbergers were chased out with their tails between their legs.

DW: Unbelievable!

BF: That's there for everybody to see.

HOW CAN THESE 80 COUNTRIES ACTUALLY DEFEAT THE CABAL?

DW: So you're saying that this meeting in Monaco took place on a ship. You have representatives from 57 countries.

You said 80 countries now have signed on to this treaty.

Now could we get into some detail about why this is so significant?

What did they talk about? How are they going to pull off doing something like this, where these entities — these five corporations — control the world's media?

Let's go into that a little bit.

ONCE THEY CAN'T PAY THEIR GOONS, THEY'RE FINISHED

BF: They don't control the world's money, you see.

Once they lose the control of their goons, the people with the guns, then that's it.

PENTAGON PATRIOTS WILL OVERTAKE CABAL MEDIA OUTLETS

At a certain point, I believe the Pentagon will probably send people in to the TV headquarters in the US.

You're going to see new faces and a totally different story coming out on your TV sets soon.

DW: That's also a very heavy statement.

ISN'T THE PENTAGON PART OF THE PROB-LEM?

What is the context of the Pentagon in light of this meeting of 57 different countries?

Wouldn't everybody in the Pentagon be part of the Bilderberg/Trilateral Commission thing?

BF: No. The Pentagon was also represented there. The Bilderberg/Trilateral Commission was not.

THE MAJOR PART OF THE PENTAGON SUP-PORTS THE ALLIANCE

DW: What percentage of the Pentagon is on the side of this alliance?

BF: I've heard that the only generals who are not on board are guys like Petraeus.

From what I've heard, most of the Joint Chiefs are now with this group.

DW: What about lower levels of the hierarchy? Like the soldiers.

BF: The lower levels are completely pissed off. They support Ron Paul — and they know that there's something totally wrong.

[DW: My own insiders have told me there is a massive struggle going on within the military between those who would arrest, detain and kill American citizens and those who would not.

The majority are rejecting the plans, roughly 80-90%, from what I heard. You can't win a battle against those odds.]

THE AMERICAN PEOPLE ARE READY FOR REVOLUTIONARY CHANGE

The opinion polls in the US show that 87 percent of

Americans don't trust Washington. That should tell you the mental state in America now.

And they are saying, "We don't want these scumbags in charge anymore." They're angry, but they're not sure who they should be angry at.

That's, I think, how the majority of Americans think.

They know there is something wrong. They know it has something to do with Wall Street and Washington.

They don't know the details, but they wish somebody would come in and do something about it.

And that is what is going to happen.

These people are going to go to jail.

THE "NEOCONS" ARE THE LEADERS OF THE CABAL

And I can tell you who the leaders are.

People like Henry Kissinger, George Bush Senior, George Bush Junior, Donald Rumsfeld, Paul Wolfowitz, and Tony Blair. We know who they are.

DW: So these are Neocons and their allies.

BF: Neocons is the label that you use for them.

That's the group that had this crazy plan that somehow they could take over the world's oil and still control the world through the 21st century.

We know who they are. When you take away that curtain, it's like the Wizard of Oz. You pull away the curtain and you see a little old man sitting at the control desk.

(crosstalk) And that's what happened when I went…

MANY MEDIA NETWORKS DON'T APPEAR TO BE NEOCON OUTLETS

DW: (crosstalk) Okay. I think most people would

admit that Fox News and News Corporation could be a shill for these guys.

But to say… you're basically saying that all the media in America, for the most part, is controlled by these folks?

Why would the media not all sound like Fox, then?

NO ONE EVER TALKS ABOUT 9/11 TRUTH

BF: How many major networks and Hollywood studios have come out with 9/11 truth? Okay?

DW: Good point.

BF: Just ask yourself that. And then you can understand.

[Henry Makow recently released explosive new testimony from a Hollywood insider who explained that all studio films are inspected and approved by the cabal before release — to insure they promote their core agenda.]

DW: So you would say…

BF: (crosstalk) Look, I have to go, but what I'm telling you is this.

WE KNOW EXACTLY WHO SPENT THE MONEY

We've found this thing called the Global Collateral Accounts. It's a codebook that shows who's been using the world's money since the end of World War II — and for what reason.

It has a list of names. For example, who financed the Vietnam War and why. All that kind of stuff.

We have these records now.

MASSIVE NUMBERS OF NEW WHISTLE-BLOWERS COMING FORWARD

We're having people abandoning that cabal like rats jumping off a sinking ship.

We have a world 'Who's Who' coming to us with information.

THIS COULD BE THE BIGGEST EVENT IN 2000 YEARS

When this happens, this is going to be, I think, ultimately the biggest thing — certainly since World War II. Possibly the biggest thing in two thousand years.

We're going to see something… an ancient cabal that has controlled humanity through murder, propaganda and bribery for possibly thousands of years.

It is going to come to an end. It's going to be something that has not happened before in the history of our planet. It's going to be incredible… basically we're talking about the end of Babylonian-style tyranny.

DW: Wow.

BF: That's how far this goes back.

VATICAN AND P2 LODGE CLAIM SECRET CONTROL SINCE JULIUS CAESAR

Certainly, the P2 Freemasonic lodge and the Vatican claim that they have controlled things in secret since the time of Julius Caesar.

DW: Wow! [Another way of saying this is the Roman Empire never really ended — it just became more covert and secretive in its exercising of power.]

BF: I went to Italy. I met them and they tried to poison me. They didn't think I would come out of Italy alive with the information they gave me — but I did.

[DW: At the time, Fulford did say these people told him about the 25,920-year precession of the equinoxes cycle. They inherited prophecies that a Golden Age would result from this cycle, and its effects, beginning after the year 2012.

They are very off-base about how the prophecy would be fulfilled, as I discuss in my new book — but they have always been keenly aware of this as their timetable, which is why there is such urgency.

Fulford didn't cover it here, but both the Rockefeller and the Rothschild factions are being forced to step down and relinquish control by this 80-country alliance. That's why no Bilderberg / CFR / Trilateral members were allowed in.

Some insiders have revealed they are already working out the terms of surrender at a very high level, and the process is quite unbearable for them — with lots of arguing and bruised egos.]

DW: Okay. A couple quick questions just to tie this off.

WHO NUKED THE BASES? WAS THIS PART OF THE MONACO ACCORDS?

Who did the underground bases, in your estimation? Who nuked them and why? Does it have any relationship with this meeting in Monaco?

BF: Yes. It was Pentagon white hats saying to the elite, "You're not going to destroy the surface of the planet and escape yourselves.

"If you're going to destroy the surface of the planet, you're going to destroy your families too. You're not going to escape."

They made it very clear to them that they are not going to be able to initiate some kind of nuclear holocaust and be able to get away with it.

DW: Right. [There is extensive evidence that the ETs will not allow them to nuke innocent civilians anyway — but they certainly keep trying.

Events like Hiroshima, Nagasaki and Fukushima are much less serious than the scope of what could be done in an all-out nuclear attack.

Given the extent to which ETs have powered down any and all Old World Order nuclear assets, it is amazing that the cabal continued to be in denial and believe they would ever be allowed to use them on any significant level.]

NOW THEY HAVE NOWHERE TO HIDE

These guys must have always thought somehow that these bases were safe. And now none of them are safe.

BF: Yes. They had their green houses, and their food supplies, and their big-screen TVs, and their supply of women.

It's like Dr. Strangelove. "We'll hide in our tunnels with our young ladies while everybody else up on the surface dies."

DW: Right.

BF: "Then we'll come out and we'll take over the planet — and breed like rabbits."

Well, that ain't gonna happen. OK?

THEY NOW HAVE DETAILED MAPS AND FILMS OF ALL THE BASES

DW: You had said on your blog that some of your people who were there in Monaco have detailed maps of these underground bases.

They know exactly where they are. And footage of the bases was shown?

BF: That's right. [The Pentagon gave this evidence to] the world governments to show, "Yes, it's true. These crazy people were planning to kill 90% of humanity."

The world's governments know this.

HOW MIGHT THIS EVENT HAPPEN — AND WHEN?

DW: Okay, so how can we expect that this event will take place? What might happen and when might it happen?

What are we looking at? What are we going into here? What will be the precursors of this?

BF: There are several possibilities.

The one I'm hearing the most, the one that the Pentagon backs, is a lawsuit that would lead to the arrest of the top cabalists.

WILCOCK'S OWN TESTIMONY OF WHAT IS EXPECTED

[DW: My own insiders expect that the dollar is about to collapse, thanks to this coordinated international effort — followed by the official declaration of bankruptcy by the US government. That will be the immediate precursor event.

I have been told the insiders are considering seven different ways in which this collapse could happen. All of them are thought to be potentially very imminent, even before the end of the year.

No one is certain of the exact timing, though, and the "windows" are always changing based on unpredictable events.

The recent announcement of the bankruptcy of the US Postal Service brings us very close to this point already — as one example.

THEY'RE PRAYING FOR CHAOS

Once this dollar collapse, government bankruptcy

is officially recognized and acknowledged by the public at large, the cabal expects riots and social upheaval.

Again, I believe they fantasize far too much about the scope and the severity of what will occur. It's undoubtedly a coping mechanism.

The cabal members desperately hope the people will turn against each other, as it is their last hope to maintain any control over the situation.

The fear-porn scenarios I have heard seem utterly fanciful — particularly since the majority of the military will turn on those who try to harm the public in any way.

Some of the technology that will be used to turn against the conspirators is highly classified and highly effective. Most people will probably never know it was used.

These "fragging" events will be "friendly fire" indeed. And Americans are not going to hand over their guns and gold.

THEY HAVE PLANTED EXPLOSIVES UNDER MANY CRITICAL BRIDGES

I did hear that cabal insiders have already planted demolition charges to blow up a large number of critical runways and bridges — isolating various geographical regions and causing food shortages for a period of time.

This massive strike, of course, will be blamed on "terrorists" hitting America at its weakest moment.

This is one of the strongest real threats we face once this epic announcement is finally made. Exposing these plans spoils any element of surprise.

So many insiders are defecting that many, if not

most of these explosives will hopefully be located — and neutralized in advance — if they haven't been already.

However, it may be unrealistic to assume that all of them will be neutralized, since they can all be detonated at the push of a button by remote control.

CRITICAL SUPPLIES WILL STILL BE DISTRIBUTED

They did hope this attack would lead to mass starvation, anarchy and chaos.

However, even with impaired land transit and airport runways, critical supplies will still get where they are needed by the focused efforts of the just — including the military.

The nationwide Eisenhower interstate system was built to be used as emergency aircraft runways, for example — and it is far too huge to be destroyed.

Helicopters do not require airstrips, either.

MASS ARRESTS

The official bankruptcy announcement, and the potential shock of widespread bridge and runway detonations, will be immediately followed by mass arrests.

This will include key staff from all three branches of government: senators, congressmen, judges and executives.

It will also include top military brass, top intelligence personnel, defense contractors, top media moguls, corporate executives, Federal Reserve Board staff, top financiers and "too big to fail" financial entities, et cetera.

Fulford has said that the Pentagon may now house these people, at least temporarily, in the very same "detention camps" they had originally planned on using against American citizens.

TRYING TO FIND A HIDING PLACE

Everyone on this list is scrambling for a place to hide. The bases near Washington DC and Denver were both quite popular due to their convenient locations.

Most of the top people had comfy, personalized living spaces already set up in these locations — with their own memorabilia, keepsakes and nostalgic items.

Many of these people have also moved their personal belongings to purported safety zones in South America — and only have a minimum number of items left in their own homes in the US.

ESCAPE FLIGHTS

I am told the cabal members have near-instant escape flights planned. The pilots and aircraft are now on 24-hour notice.

Most of these pilots will probably defect.

I also have very good intel that the personnel staffing these safety zones have already agreed to turn on them as soon as they arrive.

Pilots who do not defect are undoubtedly in mortal peril if they attempt to complete these flights.

Fulford also said the South American countries themselves have now agreed to infiltrate and disrupt these zones — and their incoming flights.

A MILLION DISPOSSESSED SOULS

Fulford has talked at length about how the number of insiders who are fearing for their lives is about a million people.

They have been scrambling around the world trying to beg, borrow or steal any land where they could have sanctuary.

They have used earthquake and weather weapons to punish countries who denied them access. This includes the Christchurch quake in New Zealand after the cabal was denied use of their lush, southernmost mega-island.

North Korea is the first country that is even considering helping them, and this development has only occurred recently.

Kim Jong II will only help them if they promise to help him regain control of South Korea. This entire plan is very unlikely to succeed.

And now, back to the recorded interview.]

THEY MAY SETTLE FOR A TRUTH AND RECONCILIATION COMMITTEE

BF: But right now, they're also trying to cut a deal.

[The international alliance is] saying, "Hey, look. If you guys will stop the nuclear terror, then maybe we'll forgive you."

It's one of those situations where so many people are involved that it is better to have a Truth and Reconciliation Committee rather than a bunch of arrests and beheadings, you know.

DW: So you're saying that these underground nuclear strikes against the bases…

BF: (crosstalk) What I'm saying is that there either will be thousands of arrests of prominent people, starting with people like Henry Kissinger…

Or else, they will cut a deal — and appear before a Truth and Reconciliation Committee in exchange for one time of forgiveness.

WHEN MIGHT THIS ALL COME TO A HEAD?

DW: Do we have a time window on when this all might come to a head?

BF: Well, it's a war. Who knows what crazy stuff they will do next?

It could be as early as this fall. It could be as late as next summer. I don't have a precise date.

DW: Okay.

BF: But I'm hearing we're pretty close now.

[DW: My own sources have said that due to the massive escalation of threat with the destruction of the two underground cities, this event could come to a head before the end of the year.

Also, highly classified documents dating back to 2008 had given a time window of December 2011 for a planned evacuation of the White House due to an "alien invasion".

So, in order to throw off these planned timetables, action is now happening very quickly.]

DID THE CABAL RETALIATE AGAINST THE RUSSIANS?

DW: Do you think the failure of the Russian airplane that had their entire hockey team onboard was in any way related to this war?

BF: It's possible. But generally, they would rather get a bunch of generals than hockey players.

There was a crash off the coast of Brazil that was involved in this, I know. But I don't know about the hockey players.

[DW: This is not what the insiders told me. I heard there is wide speculation that the Russian plane crash was a retaliatory attack.

Specifically, I was told that the average American sports fan is only about one percent as enthusiastic as the average Russian is about their hockey team.

Therefore, this plane crash was a groin kick to the Russian people, giving them a withering emotional and psychological attack.]

WHAT HAPPENS ONCE THE CABAL IS ACTU-ALLY DEFEATED?

DW: OK. So just in summary, then, could you paint a picture for us?

Let's assume that this happened. Let's assume that these 80 countries get what they want.

Just paint the picture of what happens. Where do we go as a planet, and how long is it going to take us to get there?

BF: It's just common sense. We have the technical ability to end poverty and stop environmental destruction within a year; we just don't have the institutions or the will to do it.

So instead of a fake War on Terror, aimed at financing the defense companies, forever, in a useless manner, you have some sort of huge campaign, globally: the equivalent of World War III, but a peaceful one.

Then, start telling the people the truth about their history —— which they've been lied to about so much.

IT'S GOING TO BE LIKE THE FALL OF JAPAN OR THE USSR — BUT MUCH BETTER

[We will] start building new institutions that are fair, transparent and meritocratic.

Anybody can climb the pyramid and get to the top

if they are good enough and determined enough —
instead of an inbred family group controlling it.

The people of Japan went through it at the end of
World War II. Suddenly they were told their emperor
was not a god, and that the war wasn't actually ending in victory. Soon everything was about to change.

It's going to be like that now.

Ask anyone who went through the end of the Soviet Union what it was like, and you get a pretty good
idea about what is coming.

But, unlike the end of the Soviet Union, it is not
going to be followed by hardship or poverty. It's going
to be followed by an era of unprecedented prosperity
and happiness.

OK? I've gotta go.

DW: Great. Thank you so much.

BF: Good Bye!

Transcript Source
http://tinyurl.com/3wrrkht

NESARA II

8
Address Never Given

John F. Kennedy talking about UFOs?

"My fellow Americans; people of the world; today we set forth on a journey into a new era. One age - the childhood of mankind - is ending and another age is about to begin.

The journey of which I speak is full of unknowable challenges, but I believe that all our yesterdays, all the struggles of the past, have uniquely prepared our generation to prevail.

Citizens of this Earth, we are not alone. God, in His infinite wisdom, has seen fit to populate His universe with other beings, intelligent creatures, such as ourselves.

How can I state this with such authority? In the year 1947 our military forces recovered from the dry New Mexico desert the remains of an aircraft of unknown origin. Science soon determined that this vehicle came from the far reaches of outer space. Since that time our government has made contact with the creators of that spacecraft.

Though this news may sound fantastic - and indeed alarming - I ask that you not greet it with pessimism or undue fear. I assure you, as your President, that these Beings mean us no harm.

Rather, they promise to help our nation overcome the common enemies of all mankind - tyranny, poverty, disease, and war.

We have determined that they are not foes, but friends.

Together with them we can create a better world. I cannot tell you that there will be no stumbling or missteps on the road ahead.

I believe that we have found the true destiny of the people of this great land: To lead the world into a glorious future.

In the coming days, weeks and months, we will learn more about these visitors, why they are here, and why our leaders have kept their presence a secret from you for so long.

I ask you to look to the future, not with timidity, but with courage, because we can achieve in our time the ancient vision of peace on Earth, and prosperity for all humankind.

God bless you."

9
Meetings With Extra-Terrestrials

Until now, only the Illuminati held meetings with extra-terrestrials and kept this secret from the populace by organizing projects such as "Majestic 12", where swat teams went out to visit anyone who reported even seeing an alien craft or aliens, in order to ensure that this person either agreed to keep silence, or his life, family and reputation would be destroyed. It was very effective.

Anyone who talked about the subject was laughed at. That is one of the standard ways of combating information which should not get out. Films about ETs depicted them as aggressive invaders of planet Earth with the intent of abducting humans, in order to instil fear into the hearts of mankind. They were pretty successful at that.

All this is about to change. There are thousands of craft in the skies these days, from a multitude of planets and galaxies, all eager to make our acquaintance and help us in our development.

Part of the NESARA announcement will be a government admission of past dealings with ETs and confirmation that they do exist, and that all those currently around the planet are of positive and good intent.

What is surprising is that there is so much evidence from the past of extraterrestrial activity, but neither scientists nor church officials will speak out about it. The Bible has many references to such happenings, although they did not use the words that we have today. Historical documents have depictions of spacecraft and astronauts.

The secrecy has been very successful. While we were blissfully unaware of it, top government and military officials were receiving advanced technology from the higher realms - most of which they use against us.

Actual landings were planned to happen worldwide in the Spring of 2005, but is now due about ten days after the announcement of NESARA. This will be a precursor to the "Second Coming" which will cause great consternation in the Church.

All religions have preached about it, but have never really expected it to happen in their lifetime.

Although all sacred books have stories of extraterrestrial beings and craft, oddly enough it has been ignored by all teachers of the church.

The first landing is to take place in the area of Salt Lake City, Utah (once the US military orders to shoot down space-craft have been rescinded and peace has been declared). **There will be a simultaneous landing in Vancouver, Canada, and other countries across the world, especially those where they have already been made welcome.**

The mother ships are too large to land, so shuttles will be used. The first landing is for PR purposes only and is unlikely to last more than 30 minutes.

Communication with ETs must be by telepathy and regrettably, not too may people are trained and competent in that skill at the moment. We all have to catch up on that ability. The 'landing' project is called "First Contact".

There have been many unadvertised landings in the past. Here is one extract: from a message received by James Gilliland:

"In July, 1952, we appeared at the White House. It created quite a stir. There was panic, we were met with aggression and the people were not ready. Since then there have been a myriad of films demonizing off-worlders, conditioning the minds of Earth Humanity to fear off-world visitors. They have been conditioned to believe that we came to conquer, enslave, eat Earth humans, etc, which is far from the truth. There is the belief that technology is power, those with the best technology are the ones who will be superior. In the interest of national security the UFOs must remain a se-

cret because of the immense power to be gained from back engineering. This is all in error. The real power and technology is in the hands of those who understand what real power is. **Real power serves, it empowers - never overpowers.** This understanding opens the door to the power of creation, technologies beyond your wildest dreams. These technologies will NOT be available to those without the consciousness to handle them.

"It is the same message delivered by every prophet and teacher throughout the millennium. Any other course ends in destruction, the collapse of civilization, and the very platform for life. Choosing to live by the universal principles and understandings will bring an end to war, disease, pollution and the destruction of the environment. It is the only path that will insure the continuation of this civilization. The Earth will always survive. She will reset and cleanse herself. Earth humanity has the option of starting over as primitives, losing all technology, as it has in the past or continuing forward in evolution, eventually joining the greater family of man. We are the inspiration behind the forward evolution. We cannot choose for humanity, we can only inspire, guide and in some cases protect life, for all life is precious.

"Many of your sceptics, often referred to as debunkers, already know we exist. Some have not been educated in what is outside the box of the mainstream, which is based prima-

rily on recycled ignorance.

To prove or force knowledge on them is an act of trespass. It is not in alignment with their freewill and choice which is to remain in their present understanding.

The greatest fear is of the unknown, yet when it is known it is not to be feared. In order to have contact one must rise to the occasion. Advance themselves spiritually, open the sacred senses, such as telepathy and clairaudience.

Learn to transcend the body and the personality. *When you do this we will find you. You will be like a beacon in a primitive world that needs your help. One last thing I might add. It is destiny for Earth to heal and cleanse herself. It is also destiny for Earth humanity to join the rest of the universe. During this process the skies will be filled with ships, because to do their work, in assisting with the preservation of man, it will be necessary to show themselves on occasion. It will escalate exponentially.*

There will come a time when even the hardest hearts, and the closed minded sceptics, will have to admit the obvious. *It is destiny. Remember this, it will give you strength in the days to come."*

The press in India have publicly stated that they may be the first to announce contact with extra-terrestrials. People in Eastern Europe have little difficulty in accepting ETs. It is just mainly in the "civilized", Western World that people have been white-washed into thinking that they are merely a figment of the imagination - or evil.

The prime advantage of the arrival of extra-terrestrials will be the rapid advance in technology needed to clean up the environment, to reduce and eventually eliminate the use of fossil fuels and consequent air pollution, the elimination of disease and consequent dramatic decrease in the cost of maintaining hospitals and health-care systems.

Less known is the fact that many ETs have already arrived and are standing by to assist in the replacement of government officials who are not serving the best interests of the populace.

We need to help people understand that these ETs are not malevolent, as depicted in so many films, and although many are quite different to us in appearance, they are all here to help, and we need to communicate with them, both to understand them, and explain what we are currently doing in different fields, so that they can improve our ways. Most of the time you will not realise that they are really ETs.

One of the most significant effects of contact with ETs will be the complete reorganisation of many industries, due to new, environmentally-friendly technologies. Existing industries, dependent upon petroleum products, will collapse, and new industries will take their place, without industrial cartels directing them.

Can you imagine small space-craft (shuttles or discs) whisking you from one city to another within minutes (no time for airline food)? - think about the implications.

10
A Suggested Response

The beings who are now visiting Earth are highly evolved entities from friendly civilizations throughout the galaxy. They've been observing the development and troubles of humanity on Earth for a very long time. The Bible reports contact with them in various situations over a long period of time. An old hymn calls them the Watchers and the Holy Ones!

These visitors are love-based servants of the One we all revere as our Creator God. They have our best interests at heart and have come in response to Earth's plea for assistance, and at the express invitation of a great many human beings who know of their concern for us and their readiness to be of service. The ones we are now becoming aware of are volunteers from other worlds who are working in the service wing of the **Galactic Federation**, a tremendous fleet of **star-ships** with highly trained specialists in planetary repair and decontamination, as well as expertise in government, finance, transportation, health, education, and other services.

This special organization is called the **Ashtar Command**. It operates under the direction of Ashtar Sheran, whose immediate supervisor is **Sananda - the great one whom Earth has known as Jesus of Nazareth.** (Yes, dear ones, he is very much aware of our concerns, and the plight of all peoples on Earth!)

There is absolutely nothing to fear from these visitors! They come in response to Earth's and humanity's needs, with the express permission of almighty God! They have been invited to help us out, and are not interfering with us in any way. They have, over the past fifty or more years, been in touch with some of the world's leaders, but their offers of peaceful aid have been rebuffed.

One of their conditions was that Earth's governments forsake the use of nuclear power (especially, the bomb), but the world's powers were adamant in clinging to nuclear power, whether out of fear of their enemies' cheating, or to wield greater political strength. Foolish choice!

Now a marvelous opportunity is being presented to Earth and all her peoples!

There will be new technology that will render petroleum-based power obsolete.

There will be a cleansing and renewing of land, water, and the very air we breathe. There will be restoration of physical well-being, and a just and equitable sharing of Earth's resources, so that all of humanity will be well-fed, suitably housed, and trained for work. The burdens of life will be considerably lifted, and the human family will finally acknowledge each other as equals, as brethren.

Rejoice! We are living in a New Earth, where justice and love prevail.

11
The World After NESARA

NESARA begins a huge shift in how our world society operates. We are completing a 5,000 year cycle of what the Tibetans call the *Kali Yuga*, which loosely translated means an *Age of Darkness*. We are moving into a new period of Enlightenment.

Ascended Master Saint Germain spoke to us of these times when a shift from the old age of darkness into a new period he called the Golden Age would occur. NESARA is the public beginning of the Golden Age he foretold.

From conversations with Ascended Master Saint Germain from *Unveiled Mysteries,* by Godfre Ray King (1939):

"The Divine Plan for the future of North America, is a condition of intense activity in the greatest peace, beauty, success, prosperity, spiritual illumination, and dominion. She is to carry the Christ Light, and 'Be' the Guide for the rest of the Earth, because America is to be the heart centre of the 'Golden Age', that is now dimly touching our horizon. The greater portion of the land of North America will stand for a very long time. This has been known for thousands of years, yes! — for over two hundred thousand years."

"In your beloved America, in the not so far distant future, will come forth a similar recog-

nition of the Real Inner Self, and this her people will express in high attainment. She is a Land of Light, and Her Light shall blaze forth, brilliant as the sun at noonday, among the nations of the Earth. She was a Land of Great Light, ages ago, and will again come into her spiritual heritage, for nothing shall prevent it. She is strong within her own mind and body — stronger than you think; and that strength she will exert to rise out of, and throw off from border to border, all that weighs heavily upon her at the present time.

"America has a destiny of great import to the other nations of the Earth, and Those who have watched over her for centuries still watch. Through Their protection and Love, she shall fulfil that destiny. America! We, the Ascended Host of Light, love and guard you. America! We love you.

"A similar form of perfect government will come at a later period, when you have cast off certain fetters within that hang like fungi, and sap your strength as a vampire. Beloved ones in America, be not discouraged, when the seeming dark clouds hang low. Every one of them shall show you its golden lining. Back of the cloud that seems to threaten, is the 'Crystal Pure Light of God and His Messengers, the Ascended Masters of Love and Perfection' —watching over America, the government, and her people. Again I say, 'America, we love you.'

"One by one, great awakened souls are coming forth, who will become clearly conscious of their own mighty, inherent God-Power, and such as these will be placed in all official positions of the government. They will be more interested in the welfare of America, than in their own personal ambitions and private fortunes. Thus, will another Golden Age reign upon Earth, and be maintained for an aeon."

There are other indicators that we are approaching the "shift" from the old age of darkness, to a new period of expanded possibilities for each of us.

Below is an article about Gregg Braden's research, which discusses this 'shift' from other perspectives.

Ancient cultures have predicted uplifting improvements, and a new distribution of wealth for these times, as we 'shift' out of an age of darkness and into the Golden Age.

NESARA is the pivotal public event that proclaims the beginning of the Golden Age — the Shift of the Ages.

NESARA is the beginning of many wonderful, uplifting transformations in our lives and our societies. There will be several amazing events closely following the announcement of the true NESARA law, which will expand our lives and our understandings of ourselves and our world. We will have *many* reasons to celebrate!

NESARA II

12

Geophysics Of
The Paradigm Shift

Based on *Awakening to Zero Point: The Collective Initiation,* by Gregg Braden.
This article appeared in *Atlantis Rising,* Issue #7, January 1996

Do you feel like time is "speeding up?" Are you experiencing changes in your sleep patterns and dream states, alternating periods of "black hole" sleep, with periods of intense and vivid dream activity? Have your emotions and relationships intensified? Is dejavu a common experience for you? What about the vague feeling that something is different now; that somehow, you've been through this before? You may be happy to discover, as I was, that you are not just imagining it. You are not alone. And there are very real reasons for these experiences.

Evidence is accumulating from diverse sources, to suggest that these experiences, psychological though they may be, have a physiological and geophysical component. This means that changes within the Earth's body affect our bodies, because the two are connected together in subtle ways. [through divine Mind}

So subtle, in fact, that we are mostly unaware of this "bonding", until viewed in the life or fertility cycles of many species, that are timed to the tides or full moon, or in the recently discovered magnetite, a specialized brain cell, found in abundance in the brains of mammals, (including humans), and birds, that atune to and respond to Earth's magnetic field.

Allowing homing pigeons to home in, sea creatures to navigate migration patterns, magnetite may also be the key to understanding why some people and animals are sensitive to Earthquakes before they happen, (they sense the localized anomalies in the magnetic field, known to occur in the hours and days prior to seismic events), and perhaps why sheep have been seen to sit in rows upon ley lines, natural lines of magnetic force in the Earth. So, we are tuned; and we are affected. What are the changes within the Earth affecting us?

They are cyclical, occurring in extremely long time waves, by human standards. That's one of the reasons why we are mostly unaware of them. The best place to view the clues left behind by previous cycles, is in geological record, the book kept by the Earth herself. Science knows little about how to read these cycles, or what they mean. That information may be contained in the records of the previous cultures who lived through them.

Breakthrough research comes from Gregg Braden, who has correlated the two records, and pieced together a fascinating, and, if he's right, important picture. Braden's career history and personal experiences had much to do with recognizing this new evidence. Former experience as a computer systems designer and geologist, led him to recognize the evidence of these geophysical cycles in the geologic record.

Two Near-Death Experiences at an early age, and years spent guiding tours to sacred sites throughout the world, led him to research the temples, texts, myths, and traditions of various ancient cultures.

Braden found that previous cultures had not only experienced and left records of their experience of these cycles, they found them useful for easing access to higher states of consciousness. So useful, that in between cycles, they designed and built temples, or utilized natural sites, that exhibit these same geophysical, cyclical conditions, the same ones that are in exponential transition on Earth today.

They called this point in the cycle **"The Shift of the Ages."** What's more, they left us the instructions.

Geophysical Condition #1: Earth's Rising Base Frequency

Earth's background base frequency, or "heartbeat," (called **Schumann resonanc**e, or SR), is rising dramatically. Though it varies among geographical regions, for decades the overall measurement was 7.8 cycles per second. This was once thought to be a constant; global military communications developed on this frequency. Recent reports set the rate at 8.6, and climbing. Science doesn't know why, or what to make of it. Braden found data collected by Norwegian and Russian researchers on this; it's not widely reported in the U.S. (The only reference to SR, to be found in the Seattle Library reference section, is tied to the weather. Science acknowledges SR as a sensitive indicator of temperature variations, and worldwide weather conditions. Braden believes the fluctuating SR may be a factor in the severe storms, floods, and weather of recent years.)

Geophysical Condition #2: Earth's Diminishing Magnetic Field

While Earth's "pulse" rate is rising, her magnetic field strength, on the other hand, is declining. According to Professor Bannerjee of the University of New Mexico, the field has lost up to half its intensity in the last 4,000 years. And because a forerunner of magnetic polar reversals is this field strength, Prof. Bannerjee believes that another reversal is due. Braden believes that because these cyclical Shifts are associated with reversals, Earth's geological record indicating magnetic reversals also marks previous Shifts in history. And, within the enormous time scale represented, there were quite a few of them.

The Book of Earth Past

The geological record is like one big book, whose sedimentary pages record the events of their day. Magnetic pole reversals leave their mark in the sea floor's spreading ridges; the once molten rock's iron particles aligned to the north pole as the lava cooled and hardened. Today, through core samples, we can "read" that the magnetic orientation to North shows periodic 180 degree flipping. Over a period of 76million years, 171 reversals are recorded; nine of them in past 4 million years. "My suspicion is that the magnetic flip-flop occurs very quickly, once Earth's magnetic field has diminished near the Zero Point, then slowly builds up again," says Braden.

It may happen soon, or thousands of years from now - it's impossible to pinpoint exact dates in the geological record, says Vince Migliore, editor of Geo-Monitor Newsletter. "But we know that Earth's geomagnetic field, known to fluctuate in it's intensity in the recent geologic past, is now just a fraction of what it has been historically." What is it right now, on a scale of 10, 5 being average, I asked him. The answer: 1.5! What do scientists know of the effects? According to Migliore, a common phenomenon is tremendous migration of the magnetic poles. There are reports of such magnetic anomalies, picked up by compasses, ranging up to 15 to 20 degrees away from magnetic North.

Temple Mechanics

Braden has measured many ancient temples exhibiting unusual magnetic fields and frequencies. Anecdotal reports concur: from the 1800's to the present, people have reported hearing ringing and hums, seeing strange glows, and feeling sparks from megalithic standing stones and the Great Pyramid. The latter, a mysterious and magnificent engineering feat, is, according to Braden, the only known temple to exhibit both geophysical parameters of diminished magnetics, and rising base frequency.

As a resident of New Mexico, Braden spends considerable time among the temples of the Southwest, and points out that what we, in this country, call "Indian ruins", are referred to as "temples" in other countries, and that influences the way we think about and care for these legacies. In the circular underground temples, called kivas, built by the Anasazi culture of a thousand years ago, Braden sees "tuned resonant cavities" for the purpose of eliciting various altered states of consciousness. A resonant cavity is a hollow space, the dimensions of which have a naturally occurring frequency which sets up a resonance, or harmonic feedback loop, and tunes with another frequency. "In the case of certain kivas," says Braden, "that other frequency is the human mind."

Visit to a Kiva

He tells the story of a tour of one well preserved kiva, where his group was told they couldn't play Native American cedar flutes as they had in the past. "I was looking forward to experiencing the kiva's unusual acoustics, and the meditative reverie that often results from it. But a park ranger met us, saying that musical instruments were now prohibited, because a few days prior, a visitor had died of a brain aneurysm, while blowing a conch shell in the middle of this kiva. The park wasn't willing to risk any more accidents."

My husband Paul had a much happier experience in that very same kiva. With Braden as tour guide, Paul and I spent several days hiking dusty trails, linking kivas of different dimensions, (and frequencies), to outposts and rock outcroppings, some decorated with petroglyphs. Walking through a kiva, Paul stopped and stood, listening as with his inner senses. He sat down in the middle, closed his eyes, and tuned in. It was so powerful, with such intense emotional energy, he later reported, that he moved to the kiva's edge, sat on a ledge, continued his mediation, and there had an awakening that he feels changed the course of his life.

Inner Mechanics

Is it any accident that many temples and sites known as sacred, offer a localized experience of less magnetics and/or higher frequency? In the Great Pyramid, the upper known chambers have significantly lower magnetic readings than the lower chambers, and significantly higher than normal frequencies have been measured. Braden believes that this was part of the technology developed by previous cultures, to recreate these conditions between cycles, in chambers especially designed to utilize them for initiations.

Just what effect does a lesser magnetic field and higher vibratory rate have on us? "The opportunity to more easily change the patterns that can determine how and why we love, fear, judge, feel, need, and hurt." says Braden. "Dense magnetics lock in emotional and mental patterns from generation to generation, in the morphogenetic field. With lesser magnetic fields, this seems to ease up, allowing easier access to higher states, as the cells of our body tune to, and try to match, Earth's rising base frequency like tuning forks, thereby raising our own."

Records of Previous Shifts

Legacies both written and oral, indicate that ancient cultures worldwide, have experienced the "Shifts" of previous cycles. "The ancient record keepers left us the markers for this event, what to expect, and, very importantly, a strategy for these times," says Braden. "The strategy involves making the most of the opportunity for access to higher states of consciousness, and focuses on the importance of emotions. The Essenes made a science of this. And the ancient Egyptian mystery school initiations took place in specific temples in sequence, one before the other. Each temple, and personifying temple deity, was dedicated to one aspect of the human psyche. Each aspect must be balanced prior to moving to the next level."

Initiation Rites

Why the focus on emotions? Looking through current biotech research, Braden found that our very DNA, our life codes, are affected by our emotions. The way he explains it, DNA coding options come up as 'electives' at various times, able to turn on or off. Emotions trigger specific biochemicals, which influence the chemical voltage and frequency of cells, to which molecules such as DNA respond. Therefore it is possible for our emotions to act as "switches", for "turning on" options within our DNA, to make new amino acids, (reports of spontaneous mutations are on the increase), in preparation for an evolutionary leap. Ancient wisdom, then, offers a successful strategy for life that works on many levels.

Earth as Global Temple

"We are living the completion of a cycle that began nearly 200,000 years ago, and a process of initiation that was demonstrated over 2,000 years ago." says Braden. "In past ages, through proper initiation, these special conditions were utilized for clearer access to higher states. Now we don't have to recreate them in specialized temple chambers. We don't have to go anywhere. We are living in a global initiation chamber, with these geophysical conditions occurring on a world wide scale. It's as if Earth herself, is preparing us for the next stage of evolution."

Science may be witnessing events for which there are few points of comparison, but, says Braden, "ancient traditions have preserved the understanding, that during key moments in human history, a wisdom has been offered, allowing individuals to experience rapid change without fear. This is one of those moments. This wisdom is now being passed down. Your life is preparing you for the Shift. The recorded and predicted timetable is intact. The time is now."

The Chinese say, *"may you live in interesting times."* For those frightened of change, who equate dull with secure, this is meant as a curse. Yet interesting times, if today is any indication, may also be a rare window of opportunity, a chance to get it right this time around, a collective journey, and certainly, High Adventure. It's a personal choice.

NESARA II

13

Summation

The NESARA global prosperity programmes are on the cusp of being announced and activated. One of the protected funds involved is called The Saint Germain World Trust. This fund contains deliverable precious metals and currencies worth upwards of one **quatTUORdecillion** USA dollars. The word quattuordecillion is sometimes spelled **quatROdecillion**. It means **ten thousand, thousand, thousand, thousand, thousand, thousand, thousand, thousand, thousand, thousand, thousand, million dollars**. Or $1 with forty noughts after it.

$10,000,000,000,000,000,000,000,000,000,000,000,000,000.

Amongst other projects, **this money will be used to buy out all oil corporations, banks and pharmaceutical cartels. And it will zero out (permanently cancel) all personal, corporate and national debts worldwide.**

The NESARA money was originally scheduled to be released in the year 2000, but the Bush White House and its banking and legal conspirators worldwide prevented the disbursement. And through corporate pan-global control of mainstream media outlets, nearly all knowledge of NESARA's existence was suppressed. This is now changing.

When the NESARA global prosperity programs are openly and publicly announced, they will permanently change human civilisation in every money-related way.

The whole human population will benefit from NESARA.

Earth is a most abundant planet. There is more than enough gold-backed human money currently in existence on Earth for each and every human being to be a GBP millionaire without debts of any kind. GBP = Great Britain Pound.

NESARA is about sharing the resources of the planet around fairly. And NESARA is about putting benevolent banking systems in place worldwide to deliver this monetary fairness. No individual anywhere on Earth will be beyond the reach of the NESARA wealth redistribution programs. And no individual or organization anywhere on Earth will be able to stop it.

NESARA will cancel all credit card, mortgage and other bank debt due to illegal banking and government corruption worldwide. Income tax will be abolished. A new 14% flat rate tax on non-essential new items will provide the revenue stream for national governments. There will be increased benefits for senior citizens. In the USA, there will be a return to Constitutional Law at every level of the legal system.

President George Bush Jr, Vice President Dick Cheney, and their constitutionally illegal cabal will be removed from office with immediate effect and before the end of their present term.

So will their Khazar Zionist bosses and all members of Congress. They will be replaced with constitutionally acceptable NESARA President and Vice President Designates.

There will be new Presidential and Congressional elections within 120 days of NESARA's announcement. These elections will be carefully monitored to prevent vote theft and other illegal election activities by special interest groups.

A new USA Treasury rainbow currency will come into being, backed by gold, silver, and platinum precious metals. A new USA Treasury Bank System will be initiated in alignment with Constitutional Law. The Federal Reserve Board System will be abolished. Personal financial privacy will be restored. All judges and attorneys will be retrained in Constitutional Law.

All aggressive USA government military actions worldwide will cease and global peace will be established.

Enormous sums of money will be made available for humanitarian purposes. New hitherto suppressed technologies such as free energy devices, pollution cleanup equipment and sonic healing machines will be released for the use of all.

The Cabal engineered 911 to stop NESARA's announcement which was scheduled for 10 minutes after the Twin Towers/Pentagon/PA attacks. They have continued to use and expand War Powers Act-based invasions without lawful congressional actions and would —if not foiled — declare Martial Law to declare a Dictatorship or NWO. The failure to achieve their ends...thus far... is driving them to extremes that are becoming more and more transparent as time is running out. They are losing and they know it. They will not prevail. This is due to a Divine Decree which is being implemented throughout this and planet, solar system and universe.

Dennis Kucinich, talking on Clout/Air America Radio Wed night, actually discussed what was supposed to happen on 911: "An important Announcement was scheduled which would change our economic and political systems." (He could not use the term NESARA because of the gag order, but all who know understand that is what he was describing.)

At the time of 911 attacks, a special section of the Pentagon had just been modified for higher-security protection, and that segment of the Pentagon was a special Naval Intelligence communications facility involved with NESARA's Announcement. It was the exact target of the missile attack. Transmission of codes to central banks were already in process at the time of the attack with the announcement less than 10 minutes away.

The Pennsylvania site was an underground storage for important NESARA-related documents and was an exact targeted location. At the moment of what was called a plane crash, FEMA/FBI were already standing by in the nearby woods. They then rushed out to secure the area from other investigators. No plane crashed. Each tower was attacked by a specially-prepared aircraft, modified by CIA to carry missiles and also special holographic projectors to project the illusion of the aircraft in the news releases.

The Twin Towers sub-floors held records and a lot of gold. The black ops folks had pre-installed various explosive devices and came back several weeks before 911 to install detonators and make electrical connections and circuit checks so that they could remotely trigger the explosions to take out the massive base supports and central columns, steal the gold, and kill any people around who could testify as to what they were doing. They didn't kill them all as they were in a rush to load up the gold and get it away before the explosions were detonated. So there were witnesses to each of these actions. A total of 75,000 people were actually killed in those demolitions. Certain areas were targeted to destroy records and accounts detailing liabilities of cabal firms.

The Announcement was scheduled for 10:15 AM on Sept 11, 2001...but that was 'prevented' by the Twin Towers attacks, which were planned and executed by our own gov't's black ops agents.

There are now several groups with active plans for implementing a new paradigm to replace the one of endless war and genocide being pursued by the criminals who have taken over Western civilization.

One group centered on the British empire would like to begin construction of massive free energy facilities to remove salt from sea-water and use the resulting fresh water to turn the deserts green. This group is allying itself with the Middle Eastern monarchies and plans to work simultaneously in Australia and the Arabian peninsula.

This group also wants to pay the world's deep sea fishing fleets to stop all fishing for two or three years in order to allow the oceans to replenish themselves.

A different group based in Australia but with powerful connections throughout the G7 proposes turning the deserts green by using etheric weather engineering technology.

They also plan to start cleaning up the world's most polluted sites using zeolite, an abundant mineral that absorbs toxic substances and prevents them from interacting with the environment in a harmful manner. They also have free energy technology.

A third group based on the US military-intelligence establishment proposes a 5-year swords to plowshares transformation of the Pentagon. This group has the potential to develop the over 6,000 patents that have hitherto been suppressed for "national security" reasons.

One technology they possess is anti-gravity. This would make automobiles obsolete and allow roadways to be transformed into gardens. They claim to control technology that allows the creation of portals into other dimensions.

They claim (we have not seen proof but have heard this from many credible eye-witnesses) that many so-called underground bases around the world are actual such portals.

Hopefully we will soon be able to see if this is true. If so the implications are more than mind-boggling.

This group will no doubt join forces with the various "programs" and trusts that have been fighting the Federal Reserve Board for decades.

A fourth group linking the Vatican and Russia sent us the following proposal:

We are working with leading world scientists from top prestigious institutions in Russia, they are developing many innovations:

- in the fields of energy generating (heat and/or electricity) using water as fuel,
- manufacturing new elements and isotopes from cheap materials,
- converting radioactive materials (waste) into stable condition,
- desalinating sea water to produce fresh water without any salted residuals,
- transmutation of poisonous materials into inert materials,
- municipal waste recycling,
- motors of higher power at lower consumption of electricity,
- special converters and transformers,
- earthquake prediction,
- New Approach Towards Understanding Origination of Matter and Energy in Universe from vacuum,
- many technologies for the nuclear energy industry that will be the top energy by 2050 according to EDF, and much more.

There are many technologies/projects in need of investment that are on the market, some that are about to enter in the market and some that need more years of investigation.

NESARA II

Other Publications

NESARA: National *Economic Security and Reformation Act*
http://tinyurl.com/c8u42q6

History of Banking: *An Asian Perspective*
http://tinyurl.com/boeehjl

The People's Voice: *Former Arizona Sheriff Richard Mack*
http://tinyurl.com/d62fyg3

Asset Protection: *Pure Trust Organizations*
http://tinyurl.com/btrjfqp

The Matrix As It Is: *A Different Point Of View*
http://tinyurl.com/ckrbkge

From Debt To Prosperity: *'Social Credit' Defined*
http://tinyurl.com/d2tjmw3

Give Yourself Credit: *Money Doesn't Grow On Trees*
http://tinyurl.com/d7tphuv

My Home Is My Castle: *Beware Of The Dog*
http://tinyurl.com/bmzxc2n

Commercial Redemption: *The Hidden Truth*
http://tinyurl.com/d9etg7w

Hardcore Redemption-In-Law: *Commercial Freedom And Release*
http://tinyurl.com/cl65vrz

Oil Beneath Our Feet: *America's Energy Non-Crisis*
http://tinyurl.com/btlzqxf

Untold History Of America: *Let The Truth Be Told*
http://tinyurl.com/bu9kjjc

Debtocracy: *& Odious Debt Explained*
http://tinyurl.com/cooqzuz

New Beginning Study Course: *Connect The Dots And See*
http://tinyurl.com/cxpk42p

Monitions of a Mountain Man: *Manna, Money, & Me*
http://tinyurl.com/cusgcqs

Maine Street Miracle: *Saving Yourself And America*
http://tinyurl.com/d4yktlw

Reclaim Your Sovereignty: *Take Back Your Christian Name*
http://tinyurl.com/cf5taxh

Gun Carry In The USA: Your Right To Self-defence
http://tinyurl.com/cdn3y3y

Climategate Debunked: *Big Brother, Main Stream Media*
http://tinyurl.com/d6gy2xz

Epistle to the Americans I: *What you don't know about The Income Tax*
http://tinyurl.com/d99ujzm

Epistle to the Americans II: *What you don't know about American History*
http://tinyurl.com/cnyghyz

Epistle to the Americans III: *What you don't know about Money*
http://tinyurl.com/cp8nrh8

www.ingramcontent.com/pod-product-compliance
Lightning Source LLC
Chambersburg PA
CBHW060306290526
45789CB00001B/420